PERSONAL TRAITS OF
ABRAHAM LINCOLN

PERSONAL TRAITS OF
ABRAHAM LINCOLN

Helen Nicolay

STACKPOLE
BOOKS

A Stackpole Classic Reprint, 2006

Stackpole Books
5067 Ritter Road
Mechanicsburg, PA 17055-6921
www.stackpolebooks.com

Originally published in 1912 by The Century Company, New York

Printed in the United States of America

Cover design by Wendy Reynolds

10 9 8 7 6 5 4 3 2 1

Library of Congress Cataloging-in-Publication Data

Nicolay, Helen, 1866–1954.
  Personal traits of Abraham Lincoln / Helen Nicolay.
    p. cm.
  Originally published: New York : Century Co., 1912.
  ISBN 0-8117-3347-5 (pbk. : alk. paper)
  1. Lincoln, Abraham, 1809-1865—Psychology. I. Title.

E457.2.N64 2006
973.7092—dc22

2006011301

ISBN 978-0-8117-3347-2

PREFACE

WHEN my father began collecting material to be used in his joint work with John Hay, " Abraham Lincoln: A History," he put certain things into an envelope marked " Personal Traits," meaning to make a chapter with that heading. As the work grew the items gathered under that head overflowed from one envelope into many; and at the same time it became manifest that a chapter with such a title would be out of place. Incidents illustrating Mr. Lincoln's personal traits found their rightful place elsewhere; and the authors argued that if the work as a whole did not reflect his character, it was labor lost.

PREFACE

The envelopes, bursting with their load, were put aside. My father meant at some future time, to make of the material thus collected, a smaller and more intimate volume. More pressing literary tasks, and failing health, interfered.

Unfortunately, first-hand knowledge, that could take those miscellaneous notes, personal jottings, private letters, and newspaper clippings, unrelated as the colors on a painter's palette, and blend them into an absolutely satisfactory portrait, is not a kind of knowledge to be inherited — even by a daughter who grew up in an atmosphere of devotion to Lincoln, and who, even in childhood was accorded the privilege of helping, in so far as she was able, with the details of the " History."

That experience, however, seems to put upon her a certain obligation to use these

PREFACE

notes, while it does not lessen her sense of
the perils of the task. It is a case, indeed,
where duty and something very like pre-
sumption go hand in hand.

She wishes to make acknowledgment to
Mr. Robert Lincoln for his personal kindness in help and advice; and also to the
authors whose painstaking research has
brought to light new letters and material
since " Abraham Lincoln: A History," was
published.

Washington, D. C.,
   May 31, 1912.

CONTENTS

LIST OF ILLUSTRATIONS

PERSONAL TRAITS OF
ABRAHAM LINCOLN

PERSONAL TRAITS OF ABRAHAM LINCOLN

I

THE MAN, AND HIS NATURE

TO make claim of superhuman goodness or wisdom or ability for
Abraham Lincoln is to belittle him — to
detract from the dignity of his life and
the inspiration of his example. The reason his name is on every lip, and that the
sound of it warms every heart, is that he
was so human, yet lived on a higher plane
than his fellows. That he freed an en-
slaved race and brought a long and bitter
war to an end, is impressive, but not vital
to his greatness. The fact that counts, is
that he passed through every stage of his

marvelous career, from laboring man to ruler with more than imperial power, serenely constant to one inflexible standard of right — never arrogant and never abashed, just in act, and in sympathy a brother to mankind.

Some men, born with the gift of wit, lack judgment, or persistent energy. Others, dowered with unusual sagacity, are hampered by a cold earnestness which repels confidence. Still others, afflicted with blind unreasoning energy, blunder perpetually into destructive acts of courage and daring. Lincoln had these qualities in happy combination: wit to attract and hold men, logical sense and clear vision to plan methodical action; and, best of all, that high courage which, when the golden moment came, inspired him to bold and fearless action, regardless of what others thought and careless of consequences to himself.

THE MAN AND HIS NATURE

To study his character it is not necessary to dig at the tap-root of his family tree. It is unimportant whether his ultimate ancestor was a baron who lived by robbery, or a serf yielding his oppressor unwilling tribute of sweat and blood. To invent him a proper blazon we need only cross the ax of the pioneer with the mace, the symbol of delegated authority. In blood and brain, ambition and achievement, he was one with the men who in a single century carried American civilization from the slopes of the Alleghanies to the beaches of our Pacific coast. His grandfather was killed by savages. He himself bore arms in the last Indian war of northern Illinois.

Born in a Kentucky log cabin, reared in an Indiana frontier settlement, beginning life on his own account in an Illinois village scarcely less primitive, he moved with the tide of onward progress, not as a piece of driftwood helplessly tossed by capri-

5

cious waves, but as the pilot of his self-built craft, swayed indeed, now and then, by adverse currents, but planning his own course, and making port with the precision born of rudder and compass.

In the inscrutable ways of Providence it came about that when this man was fifty years old his self-made craft became suddenly the ship of State, and his hand on the helm the deciding factor in the lives of thirty-one millions of his fellow-countrymen.

It is not enough to say that only in America could such things be. Abraham Lincoln is not explained so easily. He was not alone the product of a new land, but of the ages. Physically a wonderful organ, mentally a wonderful instrument, he was played upon by all the wonderful influences of our new continent — by the God-given freshness of the prairies, and the mystery of primeval forests shadowing secrets of an aboriginal race — also

by Spartan fortitude, Roman law, and
Christian charity, gathered in remote days
by European forebears, and brought across
the sea to flower in him under the clear
light of a sun as yet undimmed by the
miasma of civilization. And with all this
background it took more than average
human experiences to make him what he
became.

Intellectually his life divides itself into
three periods. The first, of about forty
years, beginning in the backwoods cabin,
ended with the close of his term in Congress. The second, of about ten years,
concluded with his nomination to the Presidency. The third, of about five years,
terminated at his death. Had he been
called upon to exercise the duties of President at the end of the first period, he would
not have disgraced the office, but the schooling which followed was necessary, even
with his unusual gifts, to the fulfilment of
his destiny, and the lasting good of the

American people. " First the blade, then
the ear, then the full corn in the ear."
His life was an orderly development, each
achievement preparing the way for the one
to come.

In the first period he grew, as hundreds
of his contemporaries grew, from nothing
in wisdom and worldly possessions, to an
honorable place in the material and mental
life of his time. It was the season of his
personal growth. In the second he put a
moral question before the people in terms
so ringing that they had to listen. Without conscious will on his part, but as
inevitably as the magnet draws to itself a
following, he became in those years a leader
of men, merged his individuality in that of
a cause, and became the champion of a
great idea. In the third period, when
events crowded so thickly that the half-
century he had already lived seemed but a
short time compared to the days and weeks
of his Presidency, he was called upon to

put his championship to the test — to lead his followers through doubt and tribulation, and finally to lay down his life for the faith that was in him.

History dwells on the fact that this man, who began so humbly and traveled so far, had only one scant year of schooling; and it treasures, rightly enough, a few leaves from his copy-book, and one or two doggerel verses as precious relics. Of the teachers who walked with him all the days of his youth, it says little. Yet poverty taught him the value of industry, of skill, of reputation. Labor taught him, better than books could do, his individual right to the fruits of his individual toil. Another great teacher was solitude, in whose still places he learned to think — to measure his powers, and take counsel of his own mind and heart.

But even taking into account all these, we know practically nothing of how he educated himself, or why. The force which

moves the grain of wheat to activity remains ever a mystery. We only know that
a miracle was wrought, and that by the
time this pioneer boy reached manhood the
cast of mind as well as of body, the tricks
of speech, and the spaciousness of soul,
had developed, that remained with him to
the end.

A man of many moods but great single-
ness of aim, he was complex, yet of a
strange simplicity. So natural in manner,
so free from arrogance and assumption of
power, that some could not see how grandly
he towered above them. Unable to believe
that one so placed could have come through
the fires of life unscathed, they read into
his acts subtleties and meanings which were
not there; for, with the knowledge of a
world-wise man, he kept the heart of
a child. Humble-minded, he was confident
of his own powers. Intensely practical, he
was dowered with a poet's vision, and
a poet's capacity for pain. Keen, analyt-

ical, absolutely just, he was affectionate —
and tender-hearted almost to the verge of
unreason. Fond of merriment, he was one
of the saddest men who ever lived.

Some, seeing only one side of his character, and some another, doubted and mis-
judged him. Though those nearest him
were the ones who loved him best, even they
hardly realized the measure of his greatness. Time had to demonstrate the consummate wisdom of his acts, truth had to
unearth hidden facts, and men and women
who casually judged him and passed on
had each to bring a little tribute of praise
or blame before the world could see how the
varied and apparently contradictory elements in Lincoln's nature — sadness and
gaiety, justice, logic and mercy, humility
and assurance — combined in one genial,
luminous whole; just as conflicting colors
of the spectrum fuse together into strong
white light.

II

JUST as white light, broken into component parts, dazzles an untrained eye with reds and yellows, to the exclusion of violets and indigo, without which the gaudier colors are only disturbing factors, popular estimate has laid too much stress on one of the least of Lincoln's qualities — his story-telling power; if indeed, it was a quality, and not the result of a quality — an effect, not a cause. That he was a royal story-teller there is no doubt, but legend and popular fancy have combined to distort the measure and the reason of his gift.

Sorrow and hardship darkened the earliest years of his childhood, but his was a gay and happy nature by right of birth. As a boy he loved a story for the pure fun in it; and, since he was human, liked to tell one, because in those pioneer times of few amusements and almost no books, the exercise of the faculty carried with it popularity, even more than it does to-day. Æsop's "Fables," one of the few books that fell into his hands, was a mine of wealth to such a lad, and a formative influence as well.

Grown to manhood, he faced juries by day, or appeared after nightfall before scanty groups of settlers, gathered solemn and expectant in dimly lighted log cabins to hear his views on State politics or National tariff or internal improvement. In such conditions the power of a story to rivet attention or illuminate the dismal surroundings was not to be thrown away. Later in his career he used anecdotes with telling effect to clinch an argument, or good-humoredly turn away a bore. In the stress of his Presidency they became absolutely necessary to tide over the despondency of bloody, bitter days.

That he could not have told humorous tales with the frequency rumor indicates, is self-evident. Had he done so there would have been no time to carry on the war. He himself disclaimed responsibility for more than one-sixth of those attributed to him, adding modestly that he was " only a retail dealer," who remembered a good story when he heard it. In spite of which, most of the tales invented since the days of Abraham the patriarch have been laid to his door.

The proof of his skill in telling them lies in the avidity with which people listened for and talked about them, either in criticism or praise. For of course there were good unimaginative men who could not see beyond a story to the application of it, and who failed entirely to grasp the reason for its telling. To these he seemed to be occupying his mind with frothy nothings while the country was *in extremis* — a sort of nineteenth-century Nero, without even the dignity of Nero's music and malice.

Some went so far as to remonstrate with him for his levity. They could not see that, tortured almost beyond endurance by the responsibility and the horror of the war, he was telling stories for a purpose — reaching out instinctively for something to turn the current of his thoughts even a moment, in order that he might get a firmer grasp again, and a saner outlook upon life.

" If it were not for this occasional vent I should die," he told a scandalized and protesting congressman. Then, seeing that his visitor, who had come on a serious errand, was really hurt, he lapsed with

15

characteristic suddenness into his patient gravity, and began discussing the matter in hand.

These quick transitions from grave to gay were a constant source of wonder to his friends. He seemed so possessed with merriment while it lasted, and put it aside so quickly. Laughter was to him a stimulant, and an aid to work. In a lecture, written years before, he defined it as the " joyous, universal evergreen of life." An old Springfield friend, hearing it ring out in the White House against the lurid background of war, called it, with sudden deep insight, " the President's life-preserver."

This laugh of Mr. Lincoln's was one secret of his power as a story-teller. His own enjoyment was so genuine, his realization of a situation so keen, that it exercised a power almost hypnotic over his hearers. Even the dullest saw the scene as he did while he was describing it, his

16

ANECDOTES

expressive face showing every emotion in turn. Then when the climax was reached he would lead the laughter with a heartiness that seemed to convulse his whole body. Yet a moment later the merriment died out of his eyes, lines of care descended again like a gray veil over his face, and sad and weary, he took up his burden.

Such moments of relaxation were literally snatched from toil. No man worked harder or had longer hours than he. It was the constant endeavor of his secretaries to compress his working day within reasonable limits — and his constant practice, in the kindness of his great heart, to break through rules he admitted ought to be kept, and to see people morning, noon, and night. Importunate visitors sometimes forced their way into his very bedroom, and neither midnight nor early dawn was free from prearranged interviews. Thus care was always with him; he was never allowed to forget, even had his been a

2   17

nature to forget, that there was a great war raging in the land, and that he, more than any one else, was held accountable for its course and final outcome.

Those who heard him tell his stories are fast passing away. Which of the many attributed to him are of the one-sixth he really told, and which of the five-sixths he did not tell, is in some cases already impossible to determine. Some are vouched for by unimpeachable authority ; some bear internal evidence of untruth. Careful search has brought to light less than a hundred that seem likely to be genuine. Even if he told all these and as many more, the number would be a small one, to account for such a reputation.

Concerning the quality of his stories, certain facts stand out. They were always short. Lincoln's worst enemy never accused him of telling a long story. And they never lacked point. A third characteristic is that he always took his illustrations from a life with which he was familiar. As he expressed it, he " did not care to quarry among the ancients for his figures." The life in which he grew up, the life of pioneer times, and of the small village communities which immediately followed it in the Middle West, was poor in culture and refinements of living, but strong in racy human nature. Hence overfastidious people, who liked " quarrying among the ancients," found his stories coarse. Homely, would be a truer term, for they were never coarse in spirit, even when most sordid in detail. Ethically they always pointed a clean moral. They were of the soil — strongly of the soil — but never of the charnel-house.

His story of the skunks, for example, is the tale of a man who hid behind his woodpile and saw six of these malodorous animals walking in procession to deplete his hen-house. Firing, he killed one, and when upbraided later for not exterminat-

19

ing them all, replied with feeling that he
had been six weeks getting over the effects
of shooting that one, and "reckoned he'd
let the others go."

Then there is the story of the louse on
the man's eyebrow, supposed to have been
told by Mr. Lincoln to silence a troublesome member of the Illinois legislature who
questioned the constitutionality of every
motion made. "Mr. Speaker," said Lincoln, with a quizzical smile, and a twinkle
in his deep-set eyes, "Mr. Speaker, the objection of the Member from So-and-So reminds me of an old friend of mine," and
to the merriment of his colleagues he went
on to describe a grizzled frontiersman with
shaggy overhanging brows, and spectacles, very like the objecting legislator.
One morning, on looking out of his cabin
door the old gentleman thought he saw a
squirrel frisking on a tree near the house.
He took down his gun and fired at it, but
the squirrel paid no attention. Again and

again he fired, getting more mystified and more mortified at each failure. After a round dozen shots he threw down the gun, muttering that there was "something wrong with the rifle."

"Rifle's all right," declared his son who had been watching him. "Rifle's all right, but where's your squirrel?"

"Don't you see him?" thundered the old man, pointing out the exact spot.

"No, I don't," was the candid answer. Then, turning and staring into his father's face, the boy broke into a jubilant shout. "Now I see your squirrel! You've been firing at a louse on your eyebrow."

Certainly the moral of this could not be improved upon, however coldly one may regard the subject. And these two are the most violent examples of their class.

Then there were the stories in which subjects considered either too sacred or too profane were introduced. One described a rough frontier cabin, with children running wild, and a hard-worked wife and mother, slatternly and unkempt, not overhappy perhaps, but with a woman's loyal instinct to make the best of things before a stranger. Into this setting strode an itinerant Methodist, unctious and insistent, selling Bibles as well as preaching salvation. She received him with frontier hospitality, but grew restive under questioning she deemed intrusive, and finally answered rather sharply that of course they owned a Bible. He challenged her to produce it. A search revealed nothing. The children were called to her aid, and at last one of them unearthed and held up for inspection a few tattered leaves. Protest and reproaches on the part of the visitor, but on her own stanch sticking to her colors. " She had no idea," she declared, " that they were so nearly out."

Another told of a traveler lost during a terrific thunder-storm, blundering and floundering along in thick darkness, except when vivid lightning flashes showed him trees falling around him, and the heavens apparently rent asunder. At last a flash and a crash more terrible than all the rest brought him to his knees. He was not a praying man. His petition was short and to the point. " O Lord," he gasped, " if it 's all the same to you, please give us a little more light and a little less noise! "

A third was about building a bridge across a very dangerous and rapid river. Several engineers had tried and failed, when a devout church member told the committee in charge that he had a friend who could do it. The friend was summoned. " Can you build this bridge? " they asked him. " Certainly," was the answer. " I could build a bridge to the infernal regions." The committee was not only skeptical but shocked. After the engineer had retired his friend said, " I know —— so well, he is so honest and so good a builder, that if he *says* he can build a bridge to Hades, I suppose he can; but, I must say," he added thoughtfully, " I have my doubts about the abutments on the infernal side."

The twentieth century will regard such matters more leniently than the nineteenth; certainly it is hard to see, in the light of present-day liberty, how these can be classed as license.

Many of the stories attributed to Lincoln — very likely with reason, since everybody tells them — are of the class which, through sheer excellence and much repetition, has ceased to be personal or even national property, and become part of the folk-lore of the world. " Swapping horses while crossing a stream," is an example. He gave even these his own individual touch. His story of " trying the greens on Zerah," with its subtle accusation of human nature, was his much more artistic version of the usual " try it on the dog." As he told it, the scene of the story was the neighborhood where he grew up. In the early spring, after a monotonous winter diet, the farmers there were very fond of the dish called " greens "— boiled dandelion tops, or other harmless wild leaves. On one occasion a large and greedy family sat down to a very moderate-sized dish of greens, and Zerah, the half-witted boy, whimpered at the unfair distribution of the dainty. Shortly afterward the whole household, including himself, became desperately sick, something poisonous having been gathered by mistake. All recovered, but the lesson was not lost. After that Zerah was invariably served first, with his full share, the others saying eagerly, " Try it on Zerah; if he stands it, it won't hurt the rest of us."

This is almost the only one of Mr. Lincoln's stories that shows a trace of irony. His heart was too sunny, his belief in human nature too strong, to permit accusing his fellow men, even in jest, of cruelty or meanness.

Another point is interesting. His stories never varied. He always told them the same way. Once established, the form remained unchanged to the last word and expression. Mr. A. J. Conant, who occupied a government office in Washington during the rebellion, has given us a hint of the way in which Mr. Lincoln made a story his own. He told the President a tale which the latter enjoyed and sometimes repeated, giving him due credit. This, by the way, is not the invariable custom of story-tellers. The story was about a man who hoped to become county judge, and hired a horse and buggy from his neighbor, a liveryman, in order to drive to the nominating convention held in a town some sixteen miles away. He asked the livery-stable keeper to give him the best and fastest horse he had, *explaining that he was anxious to get there early and do a*

little log-rolling before the meeting opened.
His neighbor, *being of opposing politics,*
had other views, and furnished him with a
beast which, though starting out very well,
broke down utterly. Long before he
reached his destination the convention had
adjourned, and of course he lost the nomination. Even with its head turned toward
home the poor horse could not hurry. It
was late the following afternoon before
they pulled up in front of the stable. The
candidate's anger had had time to cool,
and feeling the uselessness of recrimina-
tion, he handed the reins over to his
neighbor, only remarking: " Jones, I
see you are training this horse for the
New York market. I know you expect to
sell him for a good price to an undertaker
for a hearse-horse." In vain the owner
protested. " Don't deny it," said the
would-be judge. " I know it is true. I
know by his gait how much time you have
spent training him to go before a hearse.

But it is all labor lost, my friend. *He will never do. He is altogether too slow. He could n't get a corpse to the cemetery in time for the resurrection!*"

The words in italics show Mr. Lincoln's interpolations. Few as they are, they disclose his quick grasp of the motives of both men, and, rendering the story plausible, make it twice as amusing.

But Lincoln's stories might have been short and good and dramatically told, and forgotten in a day. Their kindliness would not have saved them, or their homely realism. Their crowning excellence lay in being always apt — told not for themselves alone, but in illustration of some point he saw and wished to make clear to others. In that sense they were not stories at all, but parables. Their teller would have been the first to disclaim any intention of preaching. He told them as simply as he did everything else in life; but mentally and spiritually he was of the line of the

28

old Hebrew poets, who had a message to deliver, and spoke it with conviction, in vivid figures of the life they knew. And just because his stories were so apt and so wonderfully told, retelling them in print after half a century is like wrenching jewels from their setting, or sea growths from ocean gardens, or anything supremely fit and right in its own place, and displaying it mutilated in utterly alien surroundings.

So short were these stories, and so charged with meaning, that anecdote melts insensibly into simile. Sometimes it is hard to fix the boundary line between them. In a letter declining an invitation to a Jefferson birthday celebration in 1859, he wrote: " I remember being once much amused at seeing two partially intoxicated men engaged in a fight with their great-coats on, which fight, after a long and rather harmless contest, ended in each having fought himself out of his own coat and into that of the other. If the two leading parties of this day are really identical with the two in the days of Jefferson and Adams, they have performed the same feat." Is this a story, or a simile?

Lincoln's early letter to his friend Joshua F. Speed, describing his predicament when he wanted to run for Congress and instead found himself sent to the nominating convention against his will, instructed to vote for his friend Baker, as leaving him " fixed a good deal like a fellow who is made a groomsman to a man that has cut him out and is marrying his own dear ' gal,' " summed up a drama and a political situation in one sentence; though not quite so vividly as did his retort to the friend who begged him to interfere in the campaign of 1864 when Republicans were quarreling among themselves, and seemed thereby in danger of losing the election. " I learned a great many years ago," was his answer, " that in a fight between husband and wife, a third party should never get between the woman's skillet and the man's ax-helve."

His mind seemed to translate every situation into dramatic form, and he became wonderfully adept in setting forth the picture he saw in a few swift words. Pages of quotation from his letters and daily conversation could be made, showing this trait. Whether it developed out of his story-telling faculty, or side by side with it, is a question more interesting than important. His answer to the New Salem election clerk that he " could make a few rabbit tracks " when that worthy inquired if he knew how to write, indicates that it was of sufficiently early origin; and in the very last public address he made, speaking of establishing loyal governments in the southern States, he used the figure of the fowl and the egg. " Concede that the new government of Louisiana is only to what it should be, as the egg is to the fowl," he said; "we shall sooner have the fowl by hatching the egg than by smashing it."

"A man watches his pear tree day after day, impatient for the ripening of the fruit. Let him attempt to force the process, and he may spoil both fruit and tree. But let him patiently wait, and the ripe pear at length falls into his lap," was his illustration of the folly of trying to hasten public opinion. He was speaking of the Emancipation Proclamation, as he was also when he gave that disconcerting answer to the committee of Chicago clergymen: "I do not want to issue a document that the whole world will see must necessarily be inoperative, like the Pope's bull against the comet!"

"I asked him what was his policy," said the Prince de Joinville, telling of an interview he once had with President Lincoln. "I have none," he replied. "I pass my life in preventing the storm from blowing down the tent, and I drive in the pegs as fast as they are pulled up." When emancipation became a " peg," he drove it home with great effect.

" Two dogs that get less eager to fight, the nearer they come together," and, " fitting the round man into the square hole," are similes recorded in the diary of Secretary Welles. Lincoln's half-humorous likening of himself at the beginning of his first term, when civil offices had to be filled and appointments made, regardless of whether war broke out or not, to " a man so busy renting rooms in one end of his house that he has no time to put out a fire burning in the other "; his discouraged remark that sending men to the Army of the Potomac was like " shoveling fleas across a barn floor — half of them never got there "; and his searching question to critics who denounced his war methods as too severe: " Would you prosecute it in future with elder-stalk squirts charged with rose-water?" are among the most graphic.

In writing to military commanders he was constantly using such figures. His admonition to "hold on with a bull-dog grip and chew and choke," has in it the very spirit of dogged fight; while his warning to General Hooker not to get his army "entangled upon the river, like an ox jumped half over a fence, and liable to be torn by dogs front and rear, without a fair chance to gore one way or kick the other," is as comprehensive as it was sound from a military point of view.

In these, as in his anecdotes, there is a noticeable absence of bitterness. After Chickamauga he did indeed speak of Rosecrans as "confused and stunned, like a duck hit on the head," but that was in the privacy of the Executive office, to one of his confidential secretaries. To the same young man he admitted that a high official, then plotting against his reëlection, would

ANECDOTES

probably, " like the blue-bottle fly, lay eggs in every rotten spot he can find," but in public he never admitted that this officer was at fault.

Had Lincoln been of a vindictive temperament, or possessed of less self-control, this dangerous power of using words might have brought about his undoing. Had it become master of his mind, instead of its servant, it could have ridden him far, making enemies at every turn. But his kindly nature held it rigorously in check. So rigorously that when, tried beyond endurance, his pent-up feelings did break the barrier and find outlet in a stinging phrase, it was worse than any blow — as when, looking down on the sleeping Army of the Potomac, he called it, in sorrow, more than in anger, " only McClellan's body-guard."

III

IN analyzing Lincoln's influence as writer and speaker, teacher and neighbor, it must be conceded that this gift of anecdote and simile, this instinct to translate situations into dramatic form, was a tremendous help in getting his views before the public in a shape to attract and hold attention. Another gift, equally valuable, developed later — during the ten years preceding his election as President. This was his art of compressing a moral truth or a guiding principle into one short and telling sentence. All three were merely different manifestations of his dominant mental quality, his strong reasoning power.

"The point — the power to hurt — of all figures lies in the truthfulness of their application," he once said, and his faculty of picturesque presentation would have availed little, had it not been for the clear perception which made the figure he used the mirror of the fact itself.

His mind went unerringly to the heart of a thing. He saw essentials, and in the light of his straightforward gaze non-essentials shriveled and disappeared. Even abstract moral questions, which to others might appear nebulous and of uncertain outline, had for him definite shape. They could be examined from all sides. He made up his mind about them only after consideration, but they were never misty. He might approach them through darkness, but never through a fog.

And clear statement of what he saw was from boyhood a passion with him. "I remember how, when a mere child, I used to get irritated when anybody talked to me

37

in a way I could not understand," he told
a friend. " I don't think I ever got angry
at anything else in my life. But that always disturbed my temper, and has, ever
since." He would puzzle far into the
night over the sayings of men who came
to talk with his father, lying sleepless until
he believed he had caught their meaning,
and then would repeat it over and over in
simple words, until he was sure he had put
it in language plain enough for any boy to
understand.

In this bit of autobiography he has told
the secret — as much of the secret as we
can ever know — of his self-education.
Given his keen moral perceptions, his passion for clear statement, his feeling for
the beauty of words, and his sense of
humor, his literary style follows as a matter of course.

Given his clear perception of the thing
he wanted to do, his direct, simple processes of reasoning usually showed him a

way to do it. The technique might be
original, but the result was effective and
satisfactory. Thus, when his flatboat lay
half submerged over a dam, with its nose
in mid-air, he freed it from water by the
simple expedient of boring a hole in its
bottom. And when his military knowledge
was not sufficient to get his company of
Black Hawk volunteers through a gate
" endwise " in terms prescribed by the
manual, his common sense prompted him
to dismiss it " for two minutes, when it will
fall in again on the other side of the gate."
Instead of running in grooves hollowed out
by custom, his mind had the tonic direct-
ness of a child's. To the day of his death
he kept the childlike attitude of heart; he
was never too old to learn.

No process seemed too tedious or too
difficult if the end was worth while.

In answer to a query received during the
campaign of 1860, he wrote:

ABRAHAM LINCOLN

Yours of the 24th, asking " the best mode of obtaining a thorough knowledge of the law," is received. The mode is very simple, though laborious and tedious. It is only to get the books and read and study them carefully. Begin with Blackstone's " Commentaries," and after reading it carefully through, say twice, take up Chitty's " Pleadings," Greenleaf's " Evidence," and Story's " Equity," etc., in succession. Work, work, work, is the main thing.

Yours very truly, A. Lincoln.

He saw no road to knowledge by way of " six easy lessons." Work, work, work, and the use of the faculties with which the Lord endowed him, were his means of success. It was after the end of his term in Congress that he applied himself with dogged energy to mastering the propositions of Euclid, because, as he said, he was not sure he knew what the word " demonstrate " meant. When he thought he had found out, he continued the practice of the law.

In the early part of his career politics and the law went hand in hand, each helping on the other. His growing prominence in politics brought him increased law practice, while the practice of law sharpened and trained his strong reasoning powers; and both callings carried him out among people where his good fellowship and wit won him hosts of friends. The same qualities which made him agreeable to his friends made him effective with a jury. At first indeed, it was his fairness and his way of putting things, more than deep legal knowledge, which counted in the court room; while in his political addresses he was merely talking to a larger and more informal jury, using practically the same methods, whether he spoke from the body of a wagon drawn up in the shade of trees, or the less unsteady footing of

the court-room floor. It was the taking,
free-and-easy manner of the Middle West.
Litigation was not complicated by ab-
struse points of law; and in politics, campaign arguments, enlivened by anecdotes,
good-natured personalities, and pungent
observations on questions of the day, made
up the popular speech.

Major Stuart, Lincoln's first law partner, did little to foster a closer application
to study in his friend. He was always
more interested in politics than in his profession. After four years this partnership came to an end, and another was
formed with Judge Stephen T. Logan, who
had lately retired from the circuit bench.
Judge Logan was a man of more studious
temperament and of keen legal mind,
and opened to Lincoln, both by precept
and example, new vistas of work and
achievement in the law. These, to his
partner's delight, and also somewhat to his
astonishment, Lincoln embraced with ar-

dor. " He would study out his case, and make about as much of it as anybody," the judge said, years afterward, with the wonder of it still upon him. " His ambition as a lawyer increased, he grew constantly . . . he got to be quite a formidable lawyer." After four years of this stimulating companionship Judge Logan had a son ready to enter the office, and in 1845 Lincoln made way for him by opening an office of his own, taking in a young and enthusiastic junior partner, Wm. H. Herndon, a business connection which remained unbroken until Lincoln's death.

Lincoln's election to the Thirtieth Congress once more enlarged his horizon. The two winters he spent in Washington, while not adding materially to his local or national fame, were of immense benefit in his personal development. They gave him opportunity to study the complex machinery of Federal government, and its relation to that of the States at first hand,

ABRAHAM LINCOLN

and, what was quite as important, a chance
to measure himself with political leaders
and representative men from all parts of
the Union.

The drudgery of congressional life;
work on committees, and haunting Departments to look after the interests of constituents, no light task in the straggling,
unpaved, and un-omnibused Washington
of the late '40's, did not fill him with
undue elation. "Being elected to Congress, though I am very grateful to our
friends for having done it, has not pleased
me as much as I expected," he wrote his
friend Speed; and to his partner he confessed that speechmaking in the House
gave him no greater thrill than speaking
elsewhere. "I was about as badly
scared, and no worse, as I am when I speak
in court." That Lincoln habitually suf-
fered the pangs described by an eloquent
preacher: "Five minutes before sermon-
time I would rather be shot than begin;

five minutes before time to close, I would rather be shot than stop," is unlikely. That he could enjoy another's speech we have abundant proof. "I just take my pen to say that Mr. Stephens of Georgia, a little, slim, pale-faced consumptive man, with a voice like Logan's, has just concluded the very best speech of an hour's length I ever heard. My old, withered, dry eyes are full of tears yet," he wrote to Herndon. After this burst of enthusiasm it is interesting to read what Stephens wrote, years later, about the impression made on him at that time by the tall member from Illinois.

"Mr. Lincoln was careful as to his manners, awkward in his speech, but was possessed of a very strong, clear, vigorous mind. He always attracted and riveted the attention of the House when he spoke. He had no model. He was a man of strong convictions, and what Carlyle would have called an earnest man. He abounded in anecdote, and socially he always kept his company in a roar of laughter."

Socially, either as member of the " mess " at Mrs. Spriggs's boarding-house near the Capitol where he lived, or as guest at Webster's breakfast parties, Lincoln could hold his own; and in debate, as we have seen, he impressed a man of Alexander H. Stephens's brilliant intellect as " strong, clear and vigorous." But it is significant that after this experience and contact with the larger minds of the day, he set himself like a schoolboy to study works of mathematics and logic. Evidently, he felt in himself a lack of the power of close and sustained reasoning.

He returned to Springfield at the end of his term in Congress, and for four years worked hard at the law; the attention he bestowed upon it being repaid by increasing practice, and an ever-growing sense of the interest and even the responsibility of his calling. His character took on a

46

graver dignity during these years, while losing nothing in geniality and charm. He was still the center of every group he joined, and still left behind him a ripple of smiles and laughter; but his friends noticed that he was less often in their company, and more and more likely to be found in the quiet of his own office. The very short autobiography written by him in 1860 to aid in preparing the campaign "life," states that "in 1854 his profession had almost superseded the thought of politics in his mind when the repeal of the Missouri Compromise roused him as he had never been before."

This was the law passed in 1820 by which Missouri was allowed to enter the Union as a slave State, on condition that thereafter slavery was to be prohibited in all remaining United States territory lying north of latitude of 36° 30', the southern boundary-line of Missouri.

As a moral question and cause of political disturbance, slavery was as old as the nation. The germ of the Union armies came across seas in the cabin of the *Mayflower*, and that of Secession lay in the hold of the Dutch slaver which sailed up the James River in 1619. Slave codes and abolition societies were in existence before our Constitution. The signers of that instrument grappled hopelessly with the anomaly of involuntary servitude in a country dedicated to freedom; and every generation of statesmen since had labored in vain to quell the growing agitation. Eli Whitney's invention of the cotton-gin in 1793 early complicated the question of morals with that of money. From being a source of perplexity and some shame to the founders of our government it had become by 1820 a burning sectional issue, threatening disruption. The Missouri Compromise postponed the final struggle forty years, but did not quiet discussion. Most of the territory still available for making new States lay north of 36° 30′, and the South did not propose to lose a political ascendancy it had long enjoyed. Its influence brought about the annexation of Texas with the resulting Mexican War, as a means of gaining new territory south of 36° 30′. This acquisition, however, only added fuel to the flame. Compromises in the Constitution, compromise in 1820, and sundry other compromises agreed upon in 1850 in the deluded hope that they would be "final," were of no avail. A plague-spot in the body politic, it grew steadily, and increased in virulence despite all palliative measures, until only the surgery of war, and Lincoln's heroic measure of emancipation could rid us of the disease.

Lincoln had grown to manhood during this time of increasing agitation, on the border land between the two systems. He had been born in a slave State, and lived, both in Indiana and Illinois, in communities dominated largely by Kentucky traditions. But these early influences did not serve to shake his inborn aversion to slavery. It was one of the moral questions he had never seen through a fog. At the age of nineteen, on his first slow flatboat voyage down to the "sugar coast" of the Mississippi River, he had abundant time to observe the unlovely details of its practical working, and to decide that it was bad. The sight of human beings chained together "like so many fish upon a trot-line," and driven and beaten for no fault of their own, made a Whig of him, when, an ambitious boy in need of friends, he lived in a town where Whig doctrines were much in disfavor. As a member of the Illinois legislature he had prepared a "protest" which only one man had the courage to sign with him; and during his single term in Congress he voted over forty times, in one form or another, for the Wilmot Proviso, which sought to

keep slavery out of the territory acquired
as a result of the war with Mexico. He had
also, while in Congress, introduced a bill
for gradual compensated emancipation of
the slaves in the District of Columbia.
He may have thought that all his interests
now centered in the law; but consciously
or unconsciously, the subject of slavery
was always near his heart.

He believed that though slavery was
evil, the Federal government had no power
to abolish it in States where it already existed; but that it did have ample authority
to exclude it from all United States ter-
ritories. The Missouri Compromise, while
not ideal, at least served to confine it
within fixed geographical bounds.

The accidents of a senate debate and
the ambition of Lincoln's fellow-townsman
suddenly precipitated the repeal of this
measure upon the country in the innocent
guise of " a bill to organize the Territory
of Nebraska." Senator Douglas, to fur-

ther his own Presidential aims, adopted
and advocated it, utterly ignoring his
previous declaration that the Missouri
Compromise was " canonized in the hearts
of the American people as a sacred thing
which no ruthless hand would ever be reck-
less enough to disturb," and not only Lincoln, but the whole country was " roused "
— the South in advocacy of it, the North
in opposition; for its effect was to open up
once again the entire question of slavery
extension.

From January to May the battle raged
in Congress; and after that, from the day
the bill finally passed until the fall elec-
tions were held, acrimonious discussion
swept the land like a whirlwind.

For Lincoln the question had a personal
as well as a moral interest. Senator
Douglas, its chief advocate, without whose
support the measure could never have become a law, was an old acquaintance; had
indeed been his political adversary for

nearly twenty years. Some said that he had been his rival in love as well.

Lincoln took no public part in the discussion until September. Meantime he was studying the question in all its bearings, historical, legal and political. Opposition newspapers accused him of " mousing about the libraries in the State House "— and the charge was perfectly true.

When he did speak it was in a new tone of authority. His statements were backed by facts, and could be proved by legislative documents. There was no lack of force in his presentation, but it was done with unwonted seriousness. He used fewer anecdotes, and cited more history; and there was a noticeable absence of the wordy fury and explosive epithets characteristic of the day. " His speeches at once attracted a more marked attention than they had ever before done," the autobiography continues. " As the canvass pro-

ceeded he was drawn to different parts of
the State. . . . He did not abandon the
law, but gave his attention by turns to
that and politics. The State agricultural
fair was at Springfield that year, and
Douglas was announced to speak there."

The agitation had already brought the
Whig and Democratic parties in Illinois
to the verge of disruption. Douglas had
been almost mobbed when he appeared in
Chicago. By common consent political
leaders hurried to Springfield from all
parts of the State, and a sort of tourna-
ment of speech-making took place, lasting
nearly a week. Douglas made a speech on
the first day. Next afternoon Lincoln answered him, speaking for more than three
hours. Neither speech was reported in
full, but the newspapers gave much space
to the meetings. One account of Lincoln's
speech gives such a graphic picture of the
scene, that quotation, even of its very bad
English, may be forgiven.

This anti-Nebraska speech of Mr. Lincoln's was the profoundest, in our opinion,
that he has made in his whole life. He felt
upon his soul the truths burn which he uttered, and all present felt that he was true
to his own soul. His feelings once or twice
swelled within and came near stifling utterance, and particularly so when he said that
the Declaration of Independence taught us
that "all men are created equal"—that by
the laws of Nature and Nature's God all men
were free — that the Nebraska Law chained
men, and that there was as much difference
between the glorious truths of the immortal
Declaration of Independence and the Nebraska Bill as there was between God and
Mammon. These are his own words. They
were spoken with emphasis, feeling, and true
eloquence. . . . We only wish others all over
the State had seen him while uttering these
truths only as Lincoln can utter a felt and
deeply felt truth. He quivered with feeling
and emotion. The whole house was as still
as death. He attacked the Nebraska Bill
with unusual warmth and energy, and all felt

that a man of strength was its enemy, and that he intended to blast it if he could by strong and manly efforts. He was most successful. The house approved . . . by loud and continuous huzzas. Women waved their white handkerchiefs. . . . Douglas felt the sting. He frequently interrupted Mr. Lincoln. . . . Mr. Lincoln exhibited Douglas in all the attitudes he could be placed in a friendly debate. He exhibited the Bill in all its aspects, to show its humbuggery and falsehoods, and when thus . . . held up to the gaze of the vast crowd, a kind of scorn and mockery was visible upon the face of the crowd, and upon the lips of the most eloquent speaker. . . . At the conclusion of this speech every man and child felt that it was unanswerable.

Two weeks later the same champions met again, and discussed the same questions at Peoria, Illinois. It is said that at the end of this debate Senator Douglas sought a friendly interview with Lincoln for the purpose of obtaining from him an agreement that neither would speak again in public before the election. Douglas had good cause to be alarmed at the unexpected power developed by his antagonist; all the strength Mr. Lincoln displayed in the next six years — the eloquence of his "lost" speech at Bloomington in 1856, the arguments used in his joint debates with Douglas in 1858, and the convincing logic of his Cooper Institute speech in 1860 — was foreshadowed in these two discourses.

With the advent of this new and deeper interest in national affairs, and the substitution of a vital moral principle for the party issues and local questions discussed in his former campaigns, can be dated the change in Lincoln's manner of speaking. The best examples of his first style were remarkable; witty, trenchant, and effective; full of droll illustrations, and not lacking in close reasoning. They were rattling good stump speeches of the kind to win tribute of applause from the other

57

side, however unwilling; summed up in an
ancient Democrat's exclamation as he beat
his hands together lustily: "I don't believe a darned thing he says, but I can't
help clapping him — he's so *pat!*"

This now gave way to increased earnestness, and to a sober presentation of his subject, clear in statement, and exact in
defining the questions at issue:

"I do not propose to question the patriotism or to assail the motives of any
man or class of men, but rather to confine myself strictly to the naked merits
of the question. I also wish to be no less
than national in all the positions I may
take, and whenever I take ground which
others have thought, or may think, narrow, sectional and dangerous to the Union,
I hope to give a reason which will appear
sufficient, at least to some, why I think
differently. And, as this subject is no
other than part and parcel of the larger
general question of domestic slavery, I wish

to make and to keep the distinction between the existing institution and the extension of it, so broad and so clear that
no honest man can misunderstand me, and
no dishonest one successfully misrepresent
me."

Historical fact and cold logic replaced
good-natured thrusts at men and events,
anecdotes gave way to axioms, and illustrations, sparingly used, were, when employed at all, forcible rather than humorous.

" If you think you can slander a woman
into loving you, or a man into voting for
you, try it till you are satisfied."

" A highwayman holds a pistol to my
ear and mutters through his teeth, ' Stand
and deliver, or I shall kill you, and then
you will be a murderer!' "

" If I saw a venomous snake crawling
in the road, any man would say I might
seize the nearest stick and kill it; but if I
found that snake in bed with my children,

that would be another question. I might hurt the children more than the snake, and it might bite them." This was used to emphasize his point that slavery could not be attacked where it already existed. " But if there was a bed newly made up, to which the children were to be taken, and it was proposed to take a batch of young snakes and put them there with them, I take it no man would say there was any question how I ought to decide." And he characterized Douglas's policy of letting each separate territory settle the moral question for itself, as " groping for some middle ground between the right and the wrong, vain as the search for a man who should be neither a living man nor a dead man."

Logic and force, an unassailable array of facts presented with great earnestness, and infrequent though sometimes gruesomely pertinent illustrations, were not, however, the only elements of strength in this second manner of Lincoln's. It was at this period that he developed that power so noticeable in his later utterances of compressing truth into short and ringing sentences, which seemed to catch up the very spirit of his argument and focus it as in a burning glass.

" No man is good enough to govern another man without that other's consent," he said in one of the earliest of these speeches.

" When the white man governs himself, that is self-government; but when he governs himself and also governs another man, that is more than self-government — that is despotism."

" No man can logically say he does n't care whether a wrong is voted up or voted down." " He cannot say people have a right to do wrong."

" He who would be no slave must consent to have no slave. Those who deny freedom to others deserve it not for themselves, and under a just God, cannot long retain it."

"Let us have faith that right makes might, and in that faith let us dare to do our duty as we understand it." This last was the closing exhortation of his Cooper Institute speech.

Battle-cries of his new faith, they were charged with an earnestness ten times more impressive than the sallies of his earlier manner. His own growth, and the majesty of his theme, were alike apparent. No longer merely a clever speaker, talking for political ends, he had received his Pentecostal touch of flame and become a teacher — a leader of men.

IV

THOUGH we have little to do with Lincoln's youth, it is unfair to leave it entirely out of the picture, since the half-faced camp at Pigeon Cove and the settlements in Indiana and Illinois where he spent his boyhood left their lasting trace on speech and habit. It was a life of democratic equality, wherein no man was much richer or wiser than his fellows; a life of open air, neighborly helpfulness and no shams, in which each individual stood or fell on his own merits. In the White House Lincoln continued to measure people and things by these unsophisticated standards of personal worth and usefulness.

ABRAHAM LINCOLN

" Every man is said to have his peculiar ambition. Whether it be true or not,
I can say, for one, that I have no other
so great as that of being truly esteemed
of my fellow men by rendering myself
worthy of their esteem," he wrote at the
age of twenty-three, in his first published
·" Address to the Voters of Sangamon
County." As a summing up of his attitude toward society it would have been
equally true on the day of his death. He
was frankly ambitious, but with a whole-
some ambition, willing good alike to himself and his neighbor. As a means to that
end he seized on every chance bit of wisdom that came his way, welcoming it as
eagerly in the White House as in the mud-
chinked log cabin, and absorbing it, not
with a scholar's thirsty love of learning
for its own sake, but for the purpose it
might serve later on.

Although the people among whom his
youth was passed were unlettered, we are

apt to dwell with undue insistence on the intellectual poverty, as we do on the physical misery, of those days. In things of the spirit and things of the body alike, the boy had enough to nourish and stimulate, though never enough to surfeit his growing needs. If we were to imagine his early life an allegorical play, and write down as *dramatis personæ* a list of the human beings and the things that influenced him, it might read something like this:

A Father.
A Good Woman.
A Sweetheart.
A Schoolmaster.
A Constable who owned a Law Book.
A Town Drunkard.
A Bully.
A Braggart.
An Indian Chief.
A Voyage down a Great River.
A few Good Books.

ABRAHAM LINCOLN

His father, although not a worldly success, was a man of good reputation and native wit. His stepmother took the boy into her big warm heart and gave him intellectual sympathy as well as physical comfort. Sweet Ann Rutledge whose early death plunged Lincoln in such grief, was a girl of greatest purity and charm; so, in the three nearest relationships of life, he had the best the world can offer.

Mentor Graham, the New Salem schoolmaster, while not the wisest of his calling, was learned enough to help him to a knowledge of grammar and surveying. Jack Kelso, disreputable town drunkard though he was, had a love of Shakspere and Burns to offset his love of drink. Jack Armstrong, leader of the Clary's Grove rowdies, fought Lincoln, felt his strength, and loved him, to the lasting good of both. Dave Turnham, constable, possibly added to the interest of his " Revised Statutes

of Indiana " by the unnecessary ceremony
with which he surrounded the volume.
Denton Offut, who bragged and blustered,
and set Lincoln in the pathway of commer-
cial venture and heavy debt; James Gentry,
local capitalist, whose substance loaded the
flatboat upon which the future emancipator floated down into the heart of slavery;
Black Hawk, the defiant old chief, whose
revolt gave Lincoln his short experience of
military service; and the chorus of neighbors and acquaintances who laughed at
his boyish stories and mock speeches, each
had a share in building his character.

As for the few books that fell into his
hands, blind chance could never have flung
together a collection so fitted to his future
needs. The Bible, Æsop's " Fables,"
" Robinson Crusoe," " The Pilgrim's Progress," a " History of the United States,"
a " Life of Washington," and Dave Turnham's cherished copy of the " Revised
Statutes of Indiana," embracing within its

67

covers the Declaration of Independence, the Constitution of the United States, and the Ordinance of 1787 with its provision excluding slavery from the Northwest Territory.

In this small but fruitful mine he delved to good purpose. He was not abnormal — only a normal boy of unusual mental gifts, with a fixed purpose to succeed, and blessed with a stepmother who systematically abetted his efforts at self-improvement. Even his father, who, owing to the family tragedy of old Abraham Lincoln's death at the hand of savages, grew up " literally without education " and as his son tells us, " never did more in the way of writing than to bunglingly sign his own name," had ambitions for the lad, chief of which was that he should learn to " cipher clean through the 'rithmetic."

So, though the path of knowledge stopped far short of a college door, it was carefully smoothed for him inside his own home. " We took particular care not to disturb him when he was reading," his step-mother told a visitor in her old age; and John Hanks, describing their youth to-gether, says: " When Abe and I returned to the house from work, he would go to the cupboard, snatch a piece of corn-bread, take a book, sit down, cock his legs up as high as his head, and read." Not a grace-ful picture, but true to the life, and, as we are informed by one who knew him well in the White House, a habit that stayed with him all his days. " Some of his greatest work in later years was done in this grotesque Western fashion, ' sitting on his shoulder blades.' "

John Hanks, and Lincoln's stepbrother, John D. Johnston, were the ones who might have filed objections; for this humoring must have looked very like favoritism in the immunity it gave from household chores. However, even they took a pride in his " smartness," although without the

faintest desire to emulate it, they lived
and died, untouched by fame.

Lincoln and Black Hawk, the Indian
Chief in our imagined list, never met.
Indeed, Lincoln's soldiering had no military result whatever, and he was the first
to ridicule it — yet the episode had its
bearing on his whole career. He once said
of himself that he was like the Hoosier
who " reckoned he liked gingerbread better
and got less of it than any man he knew ";
and at the outset of this short campaign a
particularly sweet bit of " gingerbread "
came to him in his unexpected election by
the men of his company to the honorable
office of captain. " He has not since had
any success in life which gave him so
much pleasure," he confessed in middle
age. Since a certain amount of sweet is
good for soul as well as body, this
success did him no harm; while it was a far
more important happening of the campaign
that he should be thrown into the society of

THE START IN LIFE

Major John T. Stuart, who was to be his first law partner.

Lincoln's autobiographical notes give, in briefest form, the history of the next few years. " Returning from the campaign, and encouraged by his great popularity among his immediate neighbors, he the same year ran for the legislature, and was beaten — his own precinct, however, casting its votes 277 for him and 7 against him." " This," he states, " was the only time Abraham was ever beaten on a direct vote of the people."

Lincoln was so forgetful of self, that it is refreshing occasionally to come across perfectly innocent and pardonable traces of human vanity. He was justly proud of his place in the hearts of the American people, and it gave him uncommon satisfaction to remember that with the exception of this, his earliest venture in politics, they never failed him when allowed to express their will at first hand. In this case

71

it would have been a miracle had he succeeded. He announced his candidacy just
before starting on the Black Hawk
campaign, after only a few months' resi-
dence in the county, when he was a stranger
to practically every one outside his own
precinct, and as he got back from the war
only ten days before election, he stood
small chance against men of wider acquaintance. Two years later, when he
tried again, the result was different.

The autobiography continues: " He
was now without means and out of business, but was anxious to remain with his
friends who had treated him with so much
generosity, especially as he had nothing
elsewhere to go to. He studied what he
should do — thought of learning the blacksmith trade — thought of trying to study
law — rather thought he could not succeed
at that without a better education. Before
long, strangely enough, a man offered to
sell, and did sell, to Abraham and another

as poor as himself an old stock of goods, upon credit. They opened as merchants; . . . Of course they did nothing but get deeper and deeper in debt. He was appointed postmaster at New Salem, the office being too insignificant to make his politics an objection. The store winked out. The surveyor of Sangamon offered to depute to Abraham that portion of his work which was within his part of the county. He accepted, procured a compass and chain, studied Flint and Gibson a little, and went at it. This procured bread, and kept soul and body together. The election of 1834 came, and he was then elected to the legislature by the highest vote cast for any candidate."— Here again is the note of pride.—" Major John T. Stuart, then in full practice of the law, was also elected. During the canvass, in a private conversation, he encouraged Abraham to study law. After the election he borrowed books of Stuart, took them home with him, and went at it in good earnest. He studied with nobody. He still mixed in the surveying to pay board and clothing bills. When the legislature met, the law books were dropped, but were taken up again at the end of the session. He was reëlected in 1836, 1838, and 1840. In the autumn of 1836 he obtained a law license, and on April 15, 1837, removed to Springfield and commenced the practice — his old friend Stuart taking him into partnership."

This election to the Illinois legislature was undoubtedly the great determining event in Lincoln's life. Had he lost instead of won, the world might have gained a blacksmith and lost a President. His store had just " winked out "; he was heavily in debt, and his one unreasonable creditor had attached his horse and surveying instruments for debt, literally snatching the bread out of his mouth. The four dollars a day which Illinois legislators then received must have seemed a gift from Heaven — as it was a sign to trust to instinct and brain instead of muscle for his future career.

Intellectually it removed him at once from the dull routine of village life to the companionship and rivalry of the keenest intellects gathered from all parts of the State. It taxed all his knowledge, and confronted him with new and absorbing problems.

But life was still very primitive, and in the electioneering tours which were a feature of every campaign, social as well as political qualifications went far with the voters. Candidates were expected to appear at all sorts of neighborhood gatherings, and the man who was equally equipped to turn the accidents of a horse-race or a debate on the tariff to his advantage was the man to win.

Lincoln was in his element on such occasions. He could reconcile belligerent patriots with a joke; and in quoit throwing or impromptu trials of strength his tact and his muscle were equally valuable.

Sometimes opposing candidates met unexpectedly on these tours and spent the night under the same farmhouse roof. Then it came to a trial of wits. One of Lincoln's opponents, but his personal friend (as they all were), told how Lincoln got the better of him on such an occasion. Milking-time came, and the other, anxious to array the farmer's wife on his side, took stool and pail from her hands and went to work, chuckling at the march he was stealing. But when he finished, he discovered Lincoln leaning over the fence in fruitful idleness, deep in conversation with the lady! Then and afterward, Lincoln was preëminently a practical politician.

Not a tricky politician. Principles invariably came first with him. But in all that is fair in party warfare, the shaping

of issues, the choosing of candidates, and
that intimate knowledge of local leader-
ship, and drift of feeling, he was a master.
His retentive memory gave him an unusual
grasp of political situations, while his common sense showed him ways in which to
deal with them as direct as they were novel.
Even in the early days of his legislative
experience his fellow members felt this.
" We would ride while he would walk, but
we recognized him as a master of logic."

His letters on local political topics in
Illinois are marvels of acumen and detail.
He had tables of election figures at his
tongue's end; but his crowning gift of
political diagnosis was due to his sympathy,
strange as that may seem — to his ability
to imagine himself in the " other fellow's "
place — which gave him the power to fore-
cast with uncanny accuracy what his opponents were likely to do.

Long after he left the legislature he was
a welcome guest in its party caucuses.

On invitation of some member he would
enter and take a seat, drawing around his
shoulders the shawl he sometimes wore,
cross his long legs, clasp his hands about
his knees, and listen to what was being
said. When all had finished, he would
throw aside the shawl, and rising slowly
to his full height, would begin:

"From your talk, I gather the Democrats will do so and so," stating why he
thought so. "It seems to me, if I were a
member of this body, I should do so and
so to checkmate them "— going on to indicate the moves for days ahead; making
them all so plain that his listeners won-
dered why they had not seen it that way
themselves.

V

STRAYED OR STOLEN

From a stable in Springfield on Wednesday, 18th inst., a large bay horse, star in his forehead, plainly marked with harness; supposed to be eight years old; had been shod all around, but is believed to have lost some of his shoes, and trots and paces. Any person who will take up said horse and leave information at the *Journal* Office or with the subscriber at New Salem, shall be liberally paid for their trouble.

A. LINCOLN.

THIS was a misfortune indeed, for in those days law and politics were twin vagabonds, as peripatetic as a peddler's cart. Candidates pursued votes into remote clearings, and lawyers went about their business on horseback.

The State was divided into large judicial districts. The Eighth District, for instance, in which Lincoln lived, stretched from the Illinois River eastward to the Indiana line, and almost an equal distance north and south. Twice a year the Circuit Judge, and such lawyers as happened to have cases before him, traveled around the circuit, from one county seat to another, holding court in each; and since Illinois roads were poor at best, and at worst were seas of pasty black mud, horseback riding was the most trustworthy means of locomotion.

To Lincoln, who loved the open air, and contact with people, these long rides, usually in congenial company, were very pleasant; while to his fellow travelers his good spirits and quaint observations were a source of endless delight.

Both bench and bar seem to have regarded their semi-annual pilgrimages in the light of rather gay frolics, echoes of which still come down to us, usually with Lincoln as the central figure of a jolly group. Sometimes he is chuckling over the ways of small boys, or the family cares of a duck with her brood; sometimes laughing heartily at the antics of a clothes-line full of garments filled out and set dancing by the breeze. Occasionally he rides on, moody and silent, eyes and brain alike busy with things far away. Once he reins in his horse suddenly, and turns back half a mile to pull an unfortunate pig out of the mire.— Not from love of the pig, as he informs his companions, but " just to take a pain out of his own mind."

But in spite of his fund of fun and talk there was apt to be a serious book in his scanty luggage, and his friend Leonard Swett tells us that he found time to study " to the roots " any question in which he was at the moment interested. In after years he looked back upon these circuit experiences as among the happiest of his life.

" I guess we both wish we were back in court trying cases," he said wistfully to General Butler.

The Eighth Judicial Circuit served as the setting for many of his anecdotes. It was on a stage journey in pursuit of his calling that a man offered him a cigar. Lincoln refused with polite jocularity, saying that he " had no vices." The man gave a scornful grunt and smoked in silence for a time, then blurted out, " It 's my experience that men with no vices have plaguey few virtues! "— an observation Lincoln cherished and repeated for years.

His personal habits and tastes being of the simplest, the rough quarters and often inadequate accommodations did not trouble him in the least. His friend Judge Davis only saw Lincoln angry once from such a cause. That was when they ar-

rived cold and wet at an inn late one afternoon, to find the landlord absent, and no
wood cut for a fire. Lincoln threw off
his coat, seized an ax, and chopped vigorously for an hour, while the Judge labored
with wet kindlings. When the landlord
returned he received a warm but uncomfort-
able reception.

Judge Davis took a far keener interest
in creature comforts than Lincoln, and the
latter came back from a trip in his company, laughing heartily at a retort this
interest provoked. The Judge recognized
the difficulty of catering in remote places,
and remarked on the excellence of the
beef. "You must have to kill a whole
critter when you want meat in a place like
this."

"Yes," was the landlord's laconic answer, "we never kill less than a whole
critter."

During "Court Week" each little
county town was galvanized into fic-

ABRAHAM LINCOLN

titious activity. The Judge, by virtue of his office, was given the best
room in the flimsy wooden "hotel";
but being an open-hearted Westerner,
as well as an instrument of justice,
shared it with from one to six of his
lawyer friends. The rest packed themselves into what space was left. At meal
times the Judge sat at the head of a long
table around which lawyers, jurors, witnesses, prisoners out on bail, peddlers, and
men who cared for the teams, crowded
in hungry equality. Food, though abundant, was often so badly prepared that
only the seasoning of wit and laughter with
which it was eaten saved the company
from early and dyspeptic graves.

After the meal, those not busy in court,
or in preparing cases for the morrow, adjourned to the public room, or, carrying
their chairs out on the sidewalk, tilted
luxuriously back against the hotel, and
went on swapping stories and chunks of

political wisdom; while the male residents, and farmers from the surrounding country, strolled up to take part in the symposium.

Court Week was a political as well as a legal event; for the leading lawyers either were, or had recently been, members of the legislature, and as such were called upon to explain the " loud uninterrupted groan of hard times " which newspapers were echoing from one end of the continent to the other. It behooved a man who wished to rise either in law or in politics, to be well posted and alert. Lincoln, who was witty, and a good talker besides, was sure of enthusiastic greetings wherever he went. " He brought light with him," says one writer. No wonder. He was as ready to listen as to talk; never talked about his own troubles; and never asked for help, though always ready to give it.

In the court room he strove to divest a case of every question except the vital one, giving away point after point to his opponent until he came to the one he deemed essential, and taking his stand on that. " In law it is good policy never to plead what you need not, lest you oblige yourself to prove what you cannot," was one of his maxims. He talked to a jury as he spoke to an audience, in a kindly direct way, using the subtle flattery of making them feel that they themselves were really trying the case; that he was merely helping them to formulate what they had long believed. He spoke very clearly and deliberately, using few gestures, until some anecdote became applicable, when he told it with rare dramatic force.

Knowing the necessity of holding attention, he employed language so simple that the dullest juryman could follow him; and for the same reason he rarely spoke from notes. " Notes are a bother, taking time to make, and more to hunt up afterward," he told a law student; adding that the habit of referring to them was apt to grow upon one, and always tended to tire and confuse the listeners. Notes that he used in a case involving the pension of a bent and crippled widow of a Revolutionary soldier are certainly not prolix enough to distract a jury.

" No contract.— Not professional services.— Unreasonable charge.— Money retained by Def't not given by Pl'ff.— Revolutionary War.— Describe Valley Forge privations.— Ice.— Soldier's bleeding feet.— Pl'ff's husband.— Soldier leaving home for army.— *Skin Def't.—* Close."

For the same excellent reason he rarely used a Latin word. He felt that the average juryman could not follow high-flown language in his native tongue, let alone in a dead language, and he preferred to talk with him, man to man. A colleague who relied on different methods once quoted a legal maxim and turned to him asking, " Is n't that so, Mr. Lincoln? "

ABRAHAM LINCOLN

"If that is Latin, you had better call another witness," he answered, with a touch of shortness which recalls his confession that from childhood it irritated him to hear people talk in a way he could not understand. He had little patience with men who obscured, or tried to obscure, their own trail. It reminded him, he said, of a little Frenchman out West during the "winter of the deep snow," whose "legs were so short that the seat of his trousers rubbed out his footprints as he walked."

Secretary Usher has said that Lincoln belonged to the reasoning class of men. "As a lawyer he never claimed everything for his client. . . . He was also very careful about giving personal offense, and if he had something severe to say, he would turn to his opponent, or to the person about to be referred to, and say, 'I don't like to use this language,' or, 'I am sorry that I have to be hard on that gentleman,' and therefore, what he did say, was thrice as ef-

88

fective, and very seldom wounded the person attacked."

His way with witnesses was quite marvelous. Even if hostile at the outset, they soon came under his spell and ended by wanting to please him. A boy who was subpœnaed in a case against his uncle, told how he went on the stand determined to say as little as possible. On learning his name Mr. Lincoln began asking questions. — "Was he related to his old friend?" who happened to be the boy's grandfather. The tall lawyer showed such friendly interest that before he knew it, the little witness was pouring out the whole story. He retired covered with shame, feeling he had been most disloyal; but outside the courtroom door Lincoln met him, looked at him kindly, and stopped to say that he understood — he knew he had not meant to testify against his people, but he had done right in telling all he knew, and nobody could criticize him for it. " The whole

matter was afterwards adjusted," the little story ends, "but I never forgot his
friendly and encouraging words at a time
when I needed sympathy and consolation."

Lincoln carried his love of fair play into
every detail of his profession. "Yes," he
said to a man who sought to retain him in
a questionable suit. "There is no reasonable doubt but that I can gain your case
for you. I can set a whole neighborhood
at loggerheads; I can distress a widowed
mother and her six fatherless children, and
thereby gain for you six hundred dollars,
which rightfully belongs, it appears to me,
as much to them as it does to you. I shall
not take your case, but I will give you a
little advice for nothing. You seem a
sprightly energetic man. I would advise
you to try your hand at making six hundred dollars in some other way."

After Lincoln's death some notes, evidently intended for a lecture to law stu-
dents, were found among his papers.

" Discourage litigation," said one of these.
" Persuade your neighbors to compromise
whenever you can. Point out to them how
the nominal winner is often a real loser —
in fees, expenses, and waste of time. As a
peacemaker the lawyer has a superior opportunity of being a good man. There
will still be business enough."

Yet he occasionally allowed himself the
luxury of offering his services. In the
Armstrong murder trial, the most dramatic
of all his cases, he defended the accused for
the love he bore his parents — a friendship
dating from the day Jack Armstrong, the
bully of Clary's Grove, fought the tall
stranger who had come to live in New
Salem, and felt his strength.

Joseph Jefferson, writing of his childhood, tells how in 1839 his father went to
Springfield, and relying on the patronage
of the legislature, prepared to stay all
winter. He built a little wooden theater,
but scarcely was it opened, when a revival

began in town, and excited church members had the poor little playhouse taxed out of existence. " In the midst of our trouble a young lawyer called upon the management. He had heard of the injustice, and offered, if they would place the matter in his hands, to have the license taken off, declaring that he only desired to see fair play, and would accept no fee, whether he failed or succeeded."

When the matter came to a hearing he made an elaborate argument, covering the history of acting from antiquity down, handling his subject — and his town council — with such skill that the tax was removed. Lincoln was fond of the play, and his championship loses nothing in human interest from the fact that these were probably the first good actors it had been his fortune to see; and that he anticipated a world of delight within its walls if the little wooden theater was allowed to remain.

Judge David Davis, speaking of Lincoln's rank as a lawyer, says: "In all the elements that constitute the great lawyer he had few equals. . . . He seized the strong points of a cause, and presented them with clearness and great compactness. His mind was logical and direct, and he did not indulge in extraneous discussion. Generalities and platitudes had no charms for him. An unfailing vein of humor never deserted him; and he was able to claim the attention of court and jury when the cause was the most uninteresting, by the appropriateness of his anecdotes." An Eastern lawyer once expressed the opinion that Lincoln was wasting his time in telling stories to a jury. " Don't lay that flattering unction to your soul," was his friend's rejoinder. " Lincoln is like Tansey's horse, he ' breaks to win.' "

" The framework of his mental and moral being was honesty," Judge Davis continues, " and a wrong cause was poorly defended by him. The ability which some eminent lawyers possess, of explaining away the bad points of a cause by ingenious sophistry, was denied him. In order to bring into full activity his great powers, it was necessary that he should be convinced of the right and justice of the matter which he advocated. When so convinced, whether the matter was great or small, he was usually successful."

"There is a vague popular belief that lawyers are necessarily dishonest," Lincoln wrote in his notes for a law lecture. "I say vague, because when we consider to what extent confidence and honors are reposed in and conferred upon lawyers by the people, it appears improbable that their impression of dishonesty is very distinct and vivid. Yet the impression is common, almost universal. Let no young man choosing the law for a calling for a moment yield to the popular belief — resolve to be honest at all events; and if in your own judgment you cannot be an honest lawyer,

94

resolve to be honest without being a lawyer. Choose some other occupation, rather than the one in the choosing of which you do, in advance, consent to be a knave."

He never took a case which appeared to him unjust, and if he found out that he had been mistaken, it was only with the greatest effort that he could make himself go on with it.

" Swett," he exclaimed on one occasion, turning to his associate, " the man is guilty. You defend him. I can't." Another time he said to the lawyer engaged with him, " If you can say anything for the man, do it. If I attempt it the jury will see that I think he is guilty and convict him." On still another occasion, being suddenly confronted with proof that his client was attempting fraud, he walked out of the court room and went to his hotel in deep disgust. The Judge sent a messenger to request his return. He refused.

ABRAHAM LINCOLN

" Tell the Judge," he said, " that my hands are dirty. I came over to wash them."

" Perversely honest " was the verdict, half resentful, and wholly admiring, passed upon him by his fellow lawyers.

96

VI

PAINFULLY honest also he was in money matters. Tradition has it that his initial experience in the value of money lay in being made to pull fodder three whole days at twenty-five cents a day, to pay for a rain-soaked volume. He had borrowed the book. It got wet. He payed the price of carelessness in back-breaking toil; but after that the book was his very own. " This is a world of compensation," as he wrote some forty years later.

He told Secretary Seward that he earned his first dollar by taking two travelers and their luggage out from the river

edge to a steamboat which stopped for
them, Western fashion, in midstream. For
this service each man threw a silver half-
dollar into the bottom of the boat, where
they shone very large and fair as he rowed
ashore.

The frontier value of money differed
from ours. As a symbol it meant more, as
a commodity, less. It stood for the world
the pioneer had left behind him, and all he
wished to gain, but its momentary purchas-
ing power was strangely limited. A rifle
and a strong right arm could supply more
of his immediate needs than any amount of
gold.

This fostered an undefined feeling that
money was after all a fantastic, rather than
a real thing, and accounts for certain loose
ideas about money obligations which prevailed. For instance, in the burst of confidence and exchange of promissory notes
which inaugurated Lincoln's venture as a
merchant, not a cent of money saw the

light, though signatures and I. O. U.'s were dealt around among half a dozen men, like a hand at cards.   Death, drink, and defalcation cast their consuming blight on all the other parties to the transaction, and the whole indebtedness, amounting to six or seven hundred dollars, came finally to rest upon Lincoln's shoulders.   Instead of following the prevailing fashion, taking to his heels, or claiming that failure wiped out the debt, he assumed the load, promising to pay when he could.

His neighbors, remembering how he had tramped miles to make restitution of six and a quarter cents, and had pursued a customer with a few ounces of tea after inadvertently giving short measure, felt that he took money obligations with sufficient seriousness, and agreed to wait.   Seventeen years later, long after " Honest Old Abe " had become a household word in all Sangamon County, he paid the last fraction of what he called his " National Debt."

99

The two pieces of good fortune mentioned in his autobiography, being made deputy surveyor of Sangamon County, and postmaster of New Salem, happened providentially at this time. Both were tributes to his personal worth, not to his politics, for John Calhoun, the surveyor, was an ardent Democrat, and New Salem, except when Lincoln was running for the legislature, voted systematically against the Whigs.

The only obstacle to his becoming Calhoun's deputy lay in his abysmal ignorance of surveying — a detail which Calhoun promptly overcame by lending him a textbook, which he as promptly took to his schoolmaster friend Mentor Graham. Six weeks later, haggard from application, but equipped for his new duties, he presented himself again before Calhoun.

He was made postmaster in May, 1833, and kept the situation about three years, until New Salem's population shrank to such insignificance that a postmaster was a

100

needless luxury. Popular fable locates the office " in his hat." Its principal perquisite was the privilege of reading the newspapers addressed to it — newspapers filled at that time with the debates of Webster, and Lincoln's boyhood idol, Henry Clay.

With postage at twenty-five cents, a little actual cash also passed through his hands, and this must have been gratifying in his state of poverty, even though it belonged to the Government. How sharp a line he drew between Government property and his own came to light a number of years later, when an agent of the Postoffice Department called on him in Springfield to ask for a balance of about seventeen dollars due from the defunct New Salem office. After an instant's hesitation he rose, and going to a little trunk in a corner, took from it a cotton cloth in which the exact sum was tied up. A friend who saw his face as the agent made his request, had hastily offered a loan. " I never use any

101

man's money but my own," Lincoln said quietly, after the officer took his departure.

That he had kept it through all those years of poverty, tied up in the quaint little original package, was profoundly characteristic. His methods of dealing with cash were as simple as his honesty was strict. In his lawyer days he wrote, "This is Herndon's half," in his careful legible hand upon an envelope and put into it one part of a joint fee, while the other went into his own pocket. That was all he felt called upon to do. The firm, of course, kept books, but he was rarely moved to make an entry in them. When his inconvenient sense of honesty rendered it impossible for him to go on with a case, the other " half " followed the first into his partner's envelope.

Judge Davis wrote of him: " To his honor be it said, that he never took from a client, even when his cause was gained, more than he thought the services were worth and the client could reasonably afford to pay. The people where he practised law were not rich, and his charges were always small. When he was elected President, I question whether there was a lawyer in the circuit, who had been at the bar so long a time, whose means were not larger. It did not seem to be one of the purposes of his life to accumulate a fortune. In fact, outside of his profession, he had no knowledge of the way to make money, and he never even attempted it."

"You are pauperizing this court," Judge Davis used to tell him. "You are ruining your fellows. Unless you quit this ridiculous policy we shall all have to go to farming." But Lincoln went on serenely charging as he saw fit. Once his bill was $3.50 for collecting a note of nearly $600; but politics and professional courtesy were involved, and another man made the actual collection. A client who owed him for professional services met with financial reverses, and soon after lost his hand. Lincoln returned his note, saying, " If you had the money I would not take it."

The largest fee he ever received was in the contest between the Illinois Central Railroad and McLean County over certain taxes alleged to be due from the railroad. After litigation covering two years Lincoln won the case. He presented a bill for $2,000 which the railroad refused to pay on the ground that it was excessive. Whereupon half a dozen of his lawyer friends signed a statement that in their opinion $5,000 would be a moderate charge; and he sued the railroad for that sum and got it. The story that George B. McClellan was the man who refused the original bill with the slighting remark, " That is as much as a first-class lawyer would have charged," is manifestly untrue, since McClellan was not an officer of the road, and not even in this country at the time. Parenthetically it is interesting to be told by competent authority that the same services would now command a fee of $50,000.

In the McCormick Reaper case, about which much has been written to explain and recount his first rather unfortunate meeting with Edwin M. Stanton, the fee was about $2,000. Both of these, coming to him near the time of his joint debate with Douglas, helped tide over that period of increasing fame and decreased earnings. In the decade between 1850 and 1860 his income is said to have rarely reached $3,000 a year. Before that time it was very much less.

"The matter of fees is important," he wrote in his notes for a law lecture, "far beyond the mere question of bread and butter involved." It was their moral importance he had in mind. "Properly attended to, fuller justice is done to both lawyer and client." In his theory of money, as in his theory of life, honesty was paramount.

" Don't you think I have honestly earned twenty-five dollars? " he asked the pair of opposing lawyers who were to fix the amount of the fee in a case which had gone against him. They expected to allow him at least one hundred.

As Judge Davis said, it did not seem to be one of the purposes of his life to accumulate a fortune. He said that a house in Springfield, such as he owned, and twenty thousand dollars, which he hoped to earn before his working days were over, were " all that a man ought to want."

But he had no patience with the sin of shiftlessness, no matter how patient he might be with the sinner. His letters to his stepbrother, John D. Johnston, who was born with a genius for remaining in debt, and was always asking help, were as uncompromisingly truthful as they were generous. In one of them he wrote:

ATTITUDE TOWARD MONEY

Your request for eighty dollars I do not think it best to comply with now. At the various times when I have helped you a little you have said to me, 'We can get along very well now'; but in a very short time I find you in the same difficulty again. Now, this can only happen by some defect in your conduct. What that defect is, I think I know. You are not lazy, and still you are an idler. I doubt whether, since I saw you, you have done a good whole day's work, in any one day. You do not very much dislike to work, and still you do not work much, merely because it does not seem to you that you could get much for it. This habit of uselessly wasting time is the whole difficulty; it is vastly important to you, and still more so to your children, that you should break the habit. . . . You are now in need of some money; and what I propose is, that you shall go to work, 'tooth and nail' for somebody who will give you money for it. Let father and your boys take charge of your things at home, prepare for a crop and make the crop, and you go to work for the best money wages,

or in discharge of any debt you owe, that
you can get; and, to secure you a fair re-
ward for your labor, I now promise you, that
for every dollar you will, between this and
the first of May, get for your own labor, either
in money or as your own indebtedness, I will
give you one other dollar. By this, if you
hire yourself at ten dollars a month, from
me you will get ten more, making twenty
dollars a month for your work. In this I do
not mean you shall go off to St. Louis, or
the lead mines, or the gold mines in California, but I mean for you to go at it for
the best wages you can get close to home in
Coles County. Now if you will do this you
will soon be out of debt, and, what is better,
you will have a habit that will keep you from
getting in debt again. But, if I should now
clear you out of debt, next year you would be
just as deep in as ever. You say you would
almost give your place in Heaven for seventy
or eighty dollars. Then you value your place
in Heaven very cheap, for I am sure you
can, with the offer I make, get the seventy
or eighty dollars for four or five months'

work. You say if I will furnish you the money you will deed me the land, and, if you don't pay the money back, you will deliver possession. Nonsense! If you can't now live with the land, how will you then live without it? You have always been kind to me, and I do not mean to be unkind to you. On the contrary, if you will but follow my advice, you will find it worth more than eighty times eighty dollars to you.

He watched over and cared for the interests of his father and stepmother with the same spirit, and against similar discouraging odds; and as he grew in fame, not only family letters, ill-spelt, and more fluent than logical, but letters from old neighbors, breathing patriotism and incompetence, came with their pleas for aid, and were met in his old neighborly fashion. Here is one message which he sent out into the world:

My old friend Henry Chew, the bearer of this, is in a strait for some furniture to commence housekeeping. If any person will furnish him twenty-five dollars worth, and he does not pay for it by the 1st of January next, I will.   A. LINCOLN.

He did. But sometimes bread cast upon the waters returned in its original form. An express company's envelope was found among his papers, bearing this endorsement:

September 25, 1858.
This brought me fifteen dollars without any intimation as to where it came from. It probably came from Mr. Patterson, to whom I loaned this amount a few days ago.

LINCOLN.

During his service in the legislature his campaign expenses were small enough to satisfy the most exacting. On one occasion the Whigs contributed the sum of $200 toward his personal expenses. At the end of the canvass he handed his friend Joshua F. Speed $199.25 with the request that it be returned to the subscribers. " I did not

110

need the money," he said. " I made the canvass on my own horse; my entertainment, being at the houses of friends, cost me nothing, and my only outlay was seventy-five cents for a barrel of cider which some farm-hands insisted I should treat them to."

Railroad passes were not regarded with the same covetous suspicion, then as now, and an amusing note shows his most original way of asking for a renewal.

SPRINGFIELD, ILL., Feb. 13, 1836.

R. P. Morgan, Esq.

DEAR SIR: Says Tom to John, " Here's your old rotten wheelbarrow. I've broke it, usen 'on it. I wish you would mend it, 'case I shall want to borrow it this afternoon."

Acting on this precedent, I say, " Here's your old ' chalked hat.' I wish you would take it and send me a new one, 'case I shall want to use it the first of March."

Yours truly,

A. LINCOLN.

A letter to his friend N. B. Judd, written shortly after Douglas's victory, reveals the fact that his private subscription to the Republican campaign fund in 1858 was $500. Unlike Douglas, he paid his own ordinary expenses during the canvass, " Which, being added to my loss of time and business, bears pretty heavily upon one no better off in this world's goods than I; but as I had the post of honor, it is not for me to be over-nice."

He was bitterly attacked by the New York *Herald* for accepting a check for $200 for the famous Cooper Institute speech. No public notice was taken of it, but he was sufficiently distressed to write a private letter denying that he ever charged anything for a political speech in his life, and giving the full history of the half truth on which the accusation was based.

Having simple tastes, he managed to save something from his official salary, which few Presidents have been able to do;

but this was not by virtue of changing any of his habits in regard to money getting or giving. The cashier of one of the Washington banks, meeting an old friend of Mr. Lincoln's on the street one morning, remarked "that President of yours is the oddest man alive. Why, he endorses notes for niggers!"

At the time Lincoln entered the White House, Government credit was at a perilously low ebb. Buchanan's last two Secretaries of the Treasury found difficulty in borrowing even small sums at high interest to meet Government expenses. The Civil War immediately created new and insistent demands upon the Treasury, which expanded as the months went by into financial operations greater than ever before recorded. Lincoln's crystalline simplicity in money matters seemed hardly fitted to cope with such a situation; nor did his choice of his Presidential rival, Salmon P. Chase, a man of little previous financial experience,

8   113

for Secretary of the Treasury, seem necessarily reassuring. But the good genius
which watches over our country was never
more active. This is not the place to re-
capitulate Secretary Chase's resourceful
and masterly skill in upholding our credit
at home and abroad; a management which
Evarts called "the marvel of Europe and
the admiration of our own people."

Lincoln, realizing the worth of Mr.
Chase's services, as well as his own inexperience, exercised less constant supervision
over the Treasury than over some of the
other departments. He made occasional
suggestions, but did not insist upon them;
and when Mr. Chase needed the weight of
his assistance with Congress, either in messages, or in conversation with individuals,
gave it effectively and ungrudgingly.

In the fight to make paper money legal
tender both men advocated it as a measure
of necessity, not choice; and worked for it
with unwearying devotion. A paragraph

in John Hay's diary quotes Lincoln as saying that he " thought Chase's banking system rested on a sound basis of principle ; that is, causing the capital of the country to become interested in the sustaining of the national credit. That was the principal financial measure of Mr. Chase in which he (Lincoln) had taken an especial interest."

The two were officially in perfect accord, but politically Chase was ambitious on his own account, and personally he could never understand his chief, whose whimsical remarks and Western ways seemed to him distressingly undignified.

Mr. Chase came to him one day with a report on the vast sums of paper currency already issued, and the sums still needed to pay the soldiers and carry on the Government. At the end of the dismal recital he stopped as if to say, " What can be done about it? " Lincoln with a flicker of perplexity, and another of amusement

115

crossing his sad face, looked down on his shorter companion and answered, " Well, Mr. Secretary, I don't know, unless you give your paper mill another turn." At which levity Chase almost swore, and departed in high dudgeon.

VII

JOHN HAY'S first recollection of Lincoln was of seeing him hurry into the office of his uncle, Milton Hay, waving a newspaper, and fairly quivering with excitement as he exclaimed, " This will never do! Douglas treats it as a matter of indifference, morally, whether slavery is voted down or voted up. I tell you it will never do! "

For twenty years he and Douglas had been acquaintances and opponents. He was fully aware of the effective but not always scrupulous methods by which Douglas had distanced him in fame and fortune, using office after office as stepping-stones

117

toward the goal of his ambition, the Presidency. Personally their relations were of a
neighborly, half-familiar, wholly super-
ficial sort. " I would not behave as well
as you will have to now, for twice the
money," Lincoln had told him when Douglas was made judge of the Illinois Supreme
Court, as the result of a rather questionable
political manœuver.

Lincoln knew him to be not only a wily
and astute politician, but a master-juggler
with words, who could, by mere eloquent
bullying, hypnotize his audiences into believing that black was, if not white, a very
tender gray.

Ever since Lincoln's reëntrance into politics it had been a foregone conclusion that
he would contest Douglas's reëlection in
1858, and it must be his business in this
campaign to point out the difference between white and gray of any kind.

Douglas had returned to Illinois with a
quarrel with President Buchanan on his

hands in addition to his senatorial fight. He had staked his political future on his theory of Popular Sovereignty, while the administration had advanced far beyond that ground, and now proposed to adopt the Lecompton Constitution and make Kansas a slave State whether it would or no. This quarrel, added to his fame as a speaker, drew such crowds to his meetings that mere numbers and enthusiasm seemed likely to drown all intelligent discussion. It was to offset this that Lincoln sent Douglas his challenge to joint debate.

Mr. Norman B. Judd, who carried his note to Douglas, once told my father that Lincoln asked his advice about sending the challenge, but did it in such a way that Mr. Judd saw his mind was fully made up. Mr. Judd therefore told him he thought it would be a good thing. " He then sat down in my office and wrote that note," Mr. Judd continued. " After I got the note I had very hard work to find Douglas. I hunted for him for three days before I got a chance to present it to him. When I did so finally it made him very angry; so much so that he almost insulted me. 'What do you come to me with a thing like this for?' he asked, and indulged in other equally ill-tempered remarks."

But to refuse would mean instant loss of prestige, and he named the seven towns of Ottowa, Freeport, Jonesboro', Charleston, Galesburg, Quincy, and Alton, and dates extending through August, September, and October, as places and times of meeting.

The Democrats jubilantly predicted an easy victory. Lincoln's friends, on the other hand, were not altogether sanguine, and not a few Republicans of national reputation, like Horace Greeley of the New York *Tribune*, openly favored Douglas's reëlection, on the ground that his quarrel with the administration was only a first step toward complete political regeneration.

Lincoln was sensitive to this undercurrent. It pained him that his local party friends doubted him, and it pained him still more that men of prominence were willing to jeopardize a principle for the sake of Douglas's brilliant reputation.

Both physically and intellectually the campaign proved unusually strenuous. In addition to the seven great debates each candidate made engagements to speak at meetings of his own, sometimes at several meetings a day. As Illinois is a long State, this necessitated constant traveling. Douglas had a special train, gaily decorated, and appropriately besprinkled with campaign emblems and mottoes. Lincoln, less given to display, and less plentifully supplied with funds, used any mode of conveyance that offered — farm wagon, freight train, or local — his own engine having to pull up on a siding while his rival's special flashed by in a whirl of cinders and a roar of campaign noise.

Processions and fireworks, music and

banners, greeted each in turn, until it
seemed that the whole State had turned out
to hear the debate of these intellectual
giants. In the northern counties, settled
originally by people from New England,
sentiment favored Lincoln; the southern
end upheld Douglas in his theory that
slavery was not a moral issue, but purely
a local question.

In their very first debate, in the northern end of the State, Douglas, quick to
seize an advantage, asked his antagonist
a series of questions, avowedly designed to
bring forth answers which would make him
unpopular " down in Egypt " as the pro-
slavery end of the State was called. At
their second meeting Lincoln answered
these frankly and fully, and in return asked
Douglas four questions, the second of which
was whether, in his opinion, the people of a
United States territory could, in any lawful way, against the wish of any citizen
of the United States, exclude slavery be-

fore that territory became a State. If
Douglas answered " No," he would please
the South, at the cost of denying his
own theory of Popular Sovereignty. If he
stood by his theory and answered " Yes,"
he might win the senatorship, but in doing
so he would make bitter enemies of all the
Democrats in the South.

As he had done before, in sending the
challenge, Lincoln first made up his mind
to ask this question, and then consulted his
friends. Mr. Judd and one or two others
made a hurried journey and stormed the
hotel bedroom where their candidate was
catching a few hours' sleep, waking him
at two in the morning to implore him not
to ask it, or at least to modify its form.
" If you ask it you can never be Senator,"
they assured him. The rescue party had
its journey for its pains. Lincoln, good
natured but unmoved, sitting in scanty dis-
habille on the edge of the bed from which
he had just been routed, unconscious alike

123

of anything remarkable in his personal appearance or of anything unusual in his mental attitude, replied:

"Gentlemen, I am killing larger game. If Douglas answers, he can never be President; and the battle of 1860 is worth a hundred of this."

Yet, in spite of his wonderful political insight, there is no reason to suppose he foresaw his own prominence in the battle of 1860. His power of analysis could cut mercilessly through Douglas's most involved and fantastic arabesques of argument, but neither his logic nor his poet's vision was far-reaching enough to see the place he was to hold in the history and the hearts of his native land.

"In that day I shall fight in the ranks," he wrote his friend Judd; for Douglas answered "Yes," and in spite of Lincoln's majority of 3821 in the popular vote, an antiquated apportionment gave the legislature, and consequently the senatorship, to the Democrats.

Though disappointed, Lincoln was still serene. " I am glad I made the late race," he wrote another friend. " It gave me a hearing on the great and durable question of the age, which I could have had in no other way; and though I now sink out of view, and shall be forgotten, I believe I have made some marks which will tell for the cause of civil liberty long after I am gone."

Lincoln really wanted to be Senator. He told a friend after the Presidency was practically his, that he would rather have a full term in the Senate than four years in the White House. Douglas was willing to play the political game to the verge of sharp practice in order to become President. An ironical Fate — or our country's beneficent Providence — gave each the office desired by the other. By a further irony of Fate it was Douglas himself who prolonged interest in the senatorial contest until it merged into the Presidential campaign. Having gained his senatorship he started on a tour of the slave States to make his peace with Southern voters; and in every speech he took pains to allude to Lincoln as the champion of Abolitionism, and to his views as the platform of the Republican party. In this way Lincoln was kept before the public as an authority. "You are like Byron who woke up one morning to find himself famous. People want to know about you," a Chicago editor wrote him.

The Alleghanies still separated East from West in February, 1860, when Lincoln went to New York to deliver his Cooper Institute speech. There were still people who thought of the men across the mountains as incessantly wielding bowie-knives. They had heard of Mr. Lincoln's extraordinary height, of his story-telling,

something of his early struggles. Part of
his audience that night came expecting to
see a mountebank; part from a keen interest in his speeches as reported in the newspapers. All were intensely curious. He,
on his part, was equally curious to test the
effect of his words on a representative
Eastern audience such as filled Cooper Institute to overflowing.

His hearers saw a very tall man with a
sad, strongly marked face, perfectly self-
possessed, who began his address quietly
and soberly, as though he were addressing
a court; who told not a single story, and
who used so few gestures that, as one of
his auditors expressed it, the speech might
almost have been delivered from the head
of a barrel. Yet the impressive earnestness of his manner, the power and closeness
of his reasoning, and the fairness of all the
conclusions he drew, held their absorbed
attention. Next morning's papers showed
that his speech had taken New York by

storm. In New England, where he made
a short tour before returning home, he
was heard with equal interest by working-
men and college professors. The first
recognized him as one of themselves; the
latter marveled at his finished literary
style. Only those who dreamed of bowie-
knives went away disappointed.

Lincoln's political astuteness saved him
from one pitfall of politicians — allowing
their friends to speak of them too soon
as Presidential possibilities. It was only
a few months before the actual nomination
that he sanctioned the use of his name, and
he did it then more with an idea of strength-
ening him in some future contest with
Douglas, than with reference to either
place on the National ticket. Before going East to deliver his Cooper Institute
speech, however, he had become an avowed
candidate.

Local quarrels made it appear doubtful
for a time if he could secure the delega-

tion from his own State. As failure in this would be unfortunate for his senatorial hopes, as well as for the more immediate enterprise, his presence at the Illinois State convention was deemed advisable, and he was in the hall as a spectator when John Hanks and a companion marched in bearing the rails supposed to have been made by him in pioneer days.

After witnessing the furor they created, he did not go to the Chicago convention. He felt, he said, like the boy who had " stumped " his toe, and was too big to cry, and too much hurt to laugh — he was too much of a candidate to attend, and not enough of one to stay away.

He had his nerves well in hand, but when the National Convention met, and newspapers were filled with hints that his knowledge of politics translated into indications of the drift of chances, he found himself able to do little work. He seemed rather discouraged, and remarked as he

9   129

threw himself down on the old office lounge, that " he guessed he 'd better go back to practising law."

It is said that he was playing a desultory game of ball on a vacant lot near the *Journal* office when news came that his name was before the convention. Turning to his companions with one of his queerly humorous expressions, he disappeared into the newspaper office, and soon started for home. But progress was slow. The town was too excited to allow its most illustrious citizen to walk home unaccosted, and he was still in the business section when a boy dashed down the steps of the telegraph office and charged at full speed through the crowd, shouting at the top of his youthful lungs, " Mr. Lincoln, Mr. Lincoln, you 're nominated! "

People thickened around him as if by magic, shaking his hand and every other hand within reach. For a few minutes the

central figure seemed to forget his own
part in the general rejoicing — to be only
one of the happy cheering throng. Then,
excusing himself with the remark that there
was a little woman down on Eighth Street
who would be glad to hear the news, he
went to tell her.

Next day a committee from the Chicago
convention, headed by its chairman, Mr.
Ashmun, ranged themselves around three
sides of Mr. Lincoln's modest parlor to
formally notify him of its choice. Those
who had not seen him before eyed him
curiously as he stood, tall and gaunt,
hands folded and head bent, without visible embarrassment, but absolutely devoid
of expression, while Mr. Ashmun made his
little speech.

Then, looking up, the new candidate's
eyes and smile seemed to illumine his face
as though a lamp had been suddenly kin-
dled within, and he answered in a few well-

131

chosen words, ending with a hearty,
" Now I will no longer defer the pleasure
of taking each of you by the hand." Join-
ing Mr. Ashmun he advanced upon Governor Morgan of New York, the most
imposing figure in the group. As soon as
Mr. Ashmun made the introduction Lincoln asked his height. " Six feet three,"
was the astonished answer, and the New
Yorker lapsed into disconcerting silence,
wondering what irrelevant question this
strange Presidential candidate would ask
next. But Lincoln's genial simplicity won
them all in spite of themselves, and as
they passed out one member of the committee was heard to remark to his neighbor,
" We might have done a more brilliant
thing, but we could hardly have a done a
better one."

In the East there was difference of
opinion. " We heard the result coldly
and sadly," Emerson confessed; and
Charles Francis Adams thought that no

experiment so rash had been tried in the whole history of our Government. Douglas, on the other hand, learning of the nomination, remarked with conviction. " That means business."

VIII

B EING a Presidential candidate made astonishingly little difference in Mr. Lincoln's daily habits. More people rang the bell of the plain but comfortable house on Eighth Street. He opened the door himself if no one else was there to do it. More people stayed to dinner or supper on invitation of the host or the proud hostess, sitting down to a typically abundant Western table. When he appeared upon the street people came up to shake his hand — but they had been doing that for years.

To-day it would be impossible for a man to achieve nomination without running the gauntlet of innumerable cameras.

THE CAMPAIGN SUMMER

A gentleman who visited Springfield to congratulate Mr. Lincoln " and form his personal acquaintance " ventured to ask him " for a good likeness." He replied that he had no satisfactory picture — " But then," he said, " we will walk out together, and I will sit for one." Result: one ambrotype!

The headquarters of the National Committee remained as usual in New York. No " literary bureau," or other electioneering organization existed at Springfield. The local telegraph office, an inconvenient little apartment on the second floor of an office building near the Public Square, was not even enlarged. Lincoln wrote no public letters, and made no set or impromptu speeches, with the exception of speaking a word of greeting once or twice to passing street parades. Even the strictly confidential letters in which he gave advice on points in the campaign, did not exceed a dozen in number.

The legislature not being in session, the Governor's room in the State House was set aside for his use, and here he received his visitors, coming in usually between nine and ten o'clock in the morning, bringing with him the mail he had received at his own home. His office force consisted of one quiet young secretary, who assisted him with his correspondence in the intervals of greeting visitors; and wrote wonderingly to a correspondent of his own that Mr. Lincoln's mail averaged as many as fifty letters a day.

Many of them, being merely congratulatory, needed no answer. Letters from personal friends, Mr. Lincoln acknowledged with his own hand; and in these he showed from the first considerable confidence of success. Governor Chase was the only one of his rivals in the convention to write him. His letter, among the first to arrive, gave Lincoln much pleasure. " Holding myself the humblest of all those whose names were before the convention," he wrote in reply, " I feel especial need of the assistance of all; and I am glad — very glad — of the indication that you stand ready."

Cassius M. Clay, who had hoped to be nominated for Vice-president, wrote breezily:

Well, you have cleaned us all out. The Gods favor you, and we must with good grace submit. After your nomination for the first post, my chances were of course ruined for becoming heir to your old clothes. It became necessary to choose a Vice-president from the Northeast, and of Democratic antecedents. But after Old Kentucky had come so liberally to your rescue, I think you might have complimented us with more than two votes! Still we won't quarrel with you on that account. Nature does not aggregate her gifts; and as some of us are better looking men than yourself, we must cheerfully award you the post of honor.

ABRAHAM LINCOLN

Allow me to congratulate you, and believe me truly devoted to your success, and command my poor services if needed.

One letter of congratulation, quite apart from the rest, came from an old comrade in the Black Hawk war.

RESPECTED SIR: In view of the intimacy that at one time subsisted between you and me, I deem it my duty as well as privilege, now that the intensity of the excitement of recent transactions is a little passed from you and from me, after the crowd of congratulations already received from many friends, also to offer you my heartfelt gratulation on your very exalted position in the great Republican party. No doubt but that you will become tired of the flattery of cringing selfish adulators. But I think you will know that what I say I feel. For the attachment in the Black Hawk campaign while we messed together with Johnston, Faucher, and Wyatt, when we ground our coffee in the same cup with the hatchet handle — baked

THE CAMPAIGN SUMMER

our bread on our ramrod around the same
fire — ate our fried meat off the same piece
of elm bark — slept in the same tent every
night — traveled together by day and by
night in search of the savage foe — and together scoured the tall grass on the battle-
ground of the skirmish near Gratiot's Grove
in search of the slain — with very many incidents too tedious to name — and consum-
mated in our afoot and canoe journey home,
must render us incapable of deception.
Since the time mentioned, our pursuits have
called us to operate a little apart; yours, as
you formerly hinted, to a course of political
and legal struggle; mine to agriculture and
medicine. The success that we have both
enjoyed, I am happy to know, is very encouraging. I am also glad to know, although
we must act in vastly different spheres, that
we are enlisted for the promotion of the
same great cause — the cause which, next to
revealed religion (which is humility and
love) is most dear, the cause of Liberty, as
set forth by true Republicanism and not rank
abolitionism.

Then let us go on in the discharge of duty, trusting for aid to the Great Universal Ruler. Yours truly, George M. Harrison.

Among the letters were many requests for his opinion on points of party doctrine. For these he prepared a polite form, explaining why he could not comply. There were also many letters of advice. William Cullen Bryant, whom we are wont to consider a poet rather than a politician, wrote with " the frankness of an old campaigner," to warn him against making speeches or promises — even to be chary of kind words. Joshua R. Giddings eloquently recommended John Quincy Adams as the model for an untried Westerner to follow. Such letters Lincoln answered with modest sincerity. " I appreciate the danger against which you would guard me," he wrote Bryant, " nor am I wanting in the purpose to avoid it. I thank you for the additional strength your words give me to maintain that purpose."

THE CAMPAIGN SUMMER

Requests for details of his personal life, to be used in campaign biographies, were refused as a rule; but since " lives " were sure to be published, Lincoln made exceptions and wrote with his own hand two short biographical sketches. The longer of these, covering several sheets of legal-cap, was turned over to one William Dean Howells, then unknown to fame, who wrote from it a Life of Abraham Lincoln which served its purpose and was speedily forgotten. A cautious well-wisher sent the candidate confidential word that the proof-sheets must really be searchingly examined. He was careful to certify to the young gentleman's exquisite literary taste, but hinted darkly that his anti-slavery views might color the work. Needless to say Mr. Lincoln did not appoint a committee of revision; and so far as is known, Mr. Howells's contribution to the campaign did not lose the Republican candidate any votes.

ABRAHAM LINCOLN

After two months had gone by, and
Lincoln had received no word from his
companion on the ticket, he sent him the
following characteristic little note:

Hon. Hannibal Hamlin,
MY DEAR SIR: It appears to me that
you and I ought to be acquainted, and ac-
cordingly I write this as a sort of introduction of myself to you. You first entered the
Senate during the single term I was a member of the House of Representatives, but I
have no recollection that we were introduced.
I shall be pleased to receive a line from you.

The prospect of Republican success now
appears very flattering, so far as I can perceive. Do you see anything to the contrary?
Yours truly, A. LINCOLN.

The simplicity and friendliness of this
were duplicated in the simplicity and
friendliness with which he met his visitors
— the neighbors who trusted him, political
friends who admired him, and doubters
come from afar to see what manner of

142

Westerner a freak of popular fancy had made candidate of the vigorous young Republican party. They passed in and out of his door all day long, and each felt instinctively the kindness and honesty that shone from his deeply furrowed face. That wonderful expressive face, mirthful, shrewd, melancholy, and suffused with emotion by turns; so homely in its rugged uncompromising lines, so sad in moments of repose; on occasion so tenderly beautiful in expression. Neighbors who knew it of old, loved it, though they would probably have called it ugly. Newcomers marveled at it, but soon forgot to question if it were handsome or not.

It seems odd that such a marked face could have been unknown to any one seeking him, yet there were those who met Mr. Lincoln and failed to recognize him. My father's notes tell of a stranger who asked the way to the State House. The tall man of whom he inquired said he was

143

going there himself and offered to act as guide. Then, on reaching the Governor's room, turned upon him with a merry smile and quite inimitable gesture of apology, saying, " I am Lincoln."

Artists got permission to paint his portrait, and set up their easels in the Governor's room, doing their work as well as they could for the constant interruption of callers, and the marauding forays of Mr. Lincoln's two little boys, who appeared at intervals and got inextricably mixed with the paints, to the stifled wrath of the artist. Mr. Lincoln's mild, " Boys, boys, you must n't meddle! Now run home and have your faces washed," seemed lamentably inadequate.

Jones of Cincinnati established a sculptor's studio near by, and made a bust of Mr. Lincoln, to which the candidate referred jokingly as his " mud-head." The sculptor Volk also made studies for a statue. On a certain Sunday morning he went by appointment to the house on Eighth Street to make casts of Mr. Lincoln's hands. Being asked to hold a stick, or something of the kind, he disappeared into the woodshed, the sound of sawing was heard, and he reappeared, whittling the edges of a piece of broomhandle. Mr. Volk explained that it was not necessary to trim off the edges so carefully. " Oh, well," he said, " I thought I would like to have it nice."

Presents of a symbolic nature were showered upon the candidate until the room at the State House took on the aspect of a museum. Mr. Lincoln used the axes, wedges, log-chains, and other implements as texts for explanations and anecdotes of pioneer craft; thus making them serve a double purpose in amusing his visitors and keeping the conversation away from politics.

For in all this exchange of friendly greeting, and under all the campaign enthusiasm, was a note of increasing anxiety. The South was making ugly threats. It behooved Lincoln to keep silence on party questions, and even more on the problems of national politics which loomed ever larger and darker as the summer advanced.

He was begged to issue some statement to allay the growing unrest in the South — to say something to reassure the men " honestly alarmed." " There are no such men," he answered stoutly. " It is the trick by which the South breaks down every Northern man. If I yielded to their entreaties I would go to Washington without the support of the men who now support me. I would be as powerless as a block of buckeye wood. The honest men — you are talking of honest men — will find in our platform everything I could say now, or which they would ask me to say."

So he went on talking pleasantries and pioneer days to his visitors, watching

146

meanwhile the ever-growing menace behind the circle of their friendly faces.

The anxiety took on a personal note. In
October his secretary wrote: "Among the
many things said to Mr. Lincoln by his
visitors there is nearly always an expressed
hope that he will not be so unfortunate
as were Harrison and Taylor, to be killed
off by the cares of the Presidency — or
as is sometimes hinted, by foul means. It
is astonishing how the popular sympathy
for Mr. Lincoln draws fearful forebodings
from these two examples, which, after all,
were only a natural coincidence. Not only
do visitors mention the matter, but a great
many letters have been written to Mr.
Lincoln on the subject."

Another manifestation of the same feeling was noted by the Reverend Albert Hall,
one of the pastors of Springfield, as he sat
in the Governor's room, waiting to speak
to Mr. Lincoln. "Several weeks ago," he
wrote, "two country boys came along the

dark passage that leads to his room. One of them looked in at the door, and then called to his fellow behind, saying, ' Come on, he is here.' The boys entered and he spoke to them. Immediately one of them said that it was reported in their neighborhood that he (Mr. Lincoln) had been poisoned, and their father had sent them to see if the report was true. ' And,' said the boy with all earnestness, ' Dad says you must look out and eat nothing only what your old woman cooks for you — and Mother says so too!' "

On election day the excitement under which Springfield labored reached its height about three o'clock in the afternoon, when the candidate himself appeared in the upper room in the Court House where the voting took place. He had been recognized in the street, and even the distributors of Democratic tickets had swung their hats and shouted with the rest.

As many as his townsmen as could, fol-

148

lowed him through the halls and up the
stairs, forcing themselves into the room as
he went to the voting table and deposited
the straight Republican ticket, from which
his own name had been erased. A shout
went up as he turned again toward the
door. Hemmed in as he was by friends
and enthusiasm, he could only take off his
hat, and smile as he worked his way slowly
out of the room. "And when he smiles
heartily," the local newspaper account
added, "there is something in it good to
see."

That night, after the returns began to
come in, excitement rose again in Springfield. Good news, first from near-by pre-
cincts, then from farther away, set the
crowds to cheering. Over in the lighted
State House men began to shout and dance,
and in a room across the way their wives
and daughters dispensed smiles and good
things to eat.

Lincoln meanwhile sat alone in the little

telegraph office, reading the returns as they were handed to him. Little by little accumulating majorities reported from all directions, convinced him of Republican victory. With this conviction there fell upon him an overwhelming, almost crushing sense of his coming responsibilities. The noise of rejoicing broke into the room in waves of ever increasing sound; but the successful candidate sat on alone, with head bowed, his deep-lined face sad and set — looking into the future.

IX

IN that hour Lincoln completed one of the great and characteristic acts of his life — the choice of his cabinet. He resolved to make his four principal rivals, Seward and Chase and Cameron and Bates, his chief advisers. The audacity and unworldliness of it are alike staggering.

Whether he already felt within him a power to govern men, or whether he did it from loyal obedience to the principles of representative government, knowing that nowhere else could he find men so truly representing the different elements out of which the Republican party had been made, he deliberately chose to gather them about

him and ignore the personal questions such
an act must precipitate.

Then followed the troubled months preceding his inauguration, a season for him
of anxiety and growth, in which he passed
from his second phase of teacher, to his
third of ruler and magistrate.

The South had made ugly threats before the election, now it prepared to carry
them out. South Carolina passed its Ordinance of Secession; and one by one the
other Cotton States followed her example.
Officers of the army and navy began giving
up the Government property in their
charge. The administration at Washington seemed bound in a fatal lethargy;
while Lincoln, who saw need for instant
action, could do nothing — would be powerless until after the fourth of March.

He did not doubt either the duty or
the ability of the Government to maintain
its own integrity. "That," he said, "is
not the ugly point in the matter. The

ugly point is the necessity of keeping the Government together by force, as ours should be a government of fraternity."

In December his secretary brought him a rumor that Buchanan had ordered Major Anderson to give up Fort Moultrie if it should be attacked.

" If that is true, they ought to hang him!" Lincoln exclaimed, and went on to say that only the day before he had notified General Scott to be prepared to hold or re-take the forts immediately after the Inauguration. " There can be no doubt that in any event that is good ground to live and die by," he said.

Before the end of the year he began receiving notes offering the services of State militia to uphold National authority. But nobody wanted war. " Compromise " was the word on every lip. Letters of advice came to him, thick and fast. His visitors increased in numbers and importance. The Chenery House, where most

153

of them stayed, was so crowded with strangers that "dinner," as the young secretary sadly remarked, "is worth scrambling for."

Lincoln was urged to make up his cabinet of " conservative men," one or more of them from the South. The difficulty of doing this he showed with unsparing logic in a little unsigned editorial printed in the Springfield *Journal*.

" First. Is it known that any such gentleman of character would accept a place in the cabinet?

" Second. If yea, on what terms does he surrender to Mr. Lincoln, or Mr. Lincoln to him, on the political differences between them; or do they enter upon the administration in open opposition to each other? "

Affairs of national importance, trivial tasks, and this great menace filled his days like the interwoven details of some bad dream. His cabinet had been decided upon

154

𝔉amily and 𝔖uite of the 𝔓resident 𝔈lect :

FAMILY.

HON. A. LINCOLN,

MRS. LINCOLN AND TWO CHILDREN.

ROBT. T. LINCOLN.

DR. W. S. WALLACE,

LOCKWOOD TODD

SUITE.

JOHN G. NICOLAY, Esqr., Private Secretary.
JOHN M. HAY, Esqr., Assistant Secretary,
HON. N. B. JUDD, of Illinois,
HON. DAVID DAVIS, of Illinois,
COL. E. V. SUMNER, U. S. A.
MAJ. D. HUNTER, U. S. A.

CAPT. G. W. HAZZARD, U. S. A.
COL. E. E. ELLSWORTH, of New York.
COL. WARD H. LAMON, of Illinois.
J. M. BURGESS, Esq., of Wisconsin,
GEO. O. LATHAM.

W. S. WOOD, Superintendent of Arrangements,
BURNETT FORBES, Assistant Superintendent of Arrangements.

Party accompanying Lincoln on the Journey from Springfield
to Washington

in his own mind; but many letters and
interviews, and the exercise of much tact
were necessary in offering these appointments. His inaugural had to be written,
and its tenor kept secret from the newspaper men who dogged his footsteps. His
private affairs must be put in order; the
details of his journey to Washington decided upon; and in addition, he had to
find time and grace to appear unhurried
and agreeable with even his least desirable
callers — like the " regular genuine Se-
cessionist " who sat twirling his hat in his
hands, half inclined to hide its blue cock-
ade, until Lincoln took pity on him, engaged him in bantering conversation, and
sent him away with a copy of the Lincoln-
Douglas Debates under his arm; while a
mannerless and humorless Yankee across
the room, snarled, and evidently longed for
a fight.

Lincoln found time to pay a visit of
farewell to his stepmother in Coles

County; and on the day before starting
for Washington, appeared at his old law
office to go over matters of business with
his partner Mr. Herndon. After they had
finished their talk he threw himself down
on the old lounge, and for a while neither
spoke. He seemed to be passing in review
the incidents of his law practice; but he
was neither sad nor sentimental. Pres-
ently he began to speak of amusing
things that had happened on the Eighth
Circuit. It was only as he was taking his
leave that he paused on the threshold, and
with a sudden change of tone, asked that
the office sign be allowed to hang undisturbed. "Give our clients to understand
that the election of a President makes no
difference," he said. "If I live I'm coming back sometime, and we'll go right on
practising law, as if nothing had happened."

But how deeply he was moved by this
departure from his old home, his speech

of farewell, made from the platform of the train, as his neighbors stood uncovered in the falling snow, amply testified. There was in it a sadness and a pathos almost prophetic.

" My friends: No one not in my situation, can appreciate my feeling of sadness at this parting. To this place, and the kindness of these people, I owe everything. Here I have lived a quarter of a century, and have passed from a young to an old man. Here my children have been born, and one is buried. I now leave, not knowing when or whether ever I may return, with a task before me greater than that which rested upon Washington. Without the assistance of that Divine Being who ever attended him, I cannot succeed. With that assistance I cannot fail. Trusting in Him who can go with me, and remain with you, and be everywhere for good, let us confidently hope that all will yet be well. To His care commending you, as I hope in your prayers you will commend me, I bid you an affectionate farewell."

It was true that he went to assume a responsibility " greater than that which rested upon Washington," yet the glamour of that journey with its cheering thousands, when the train seemed to be rushing through one continuous crowd, and every throat was calling his name, might have justified even a modest man in the belief that he was to have an easy task. Lincoln accepted the acclaim in his heart, as he acknowledged it in his speeches, as a welcome from the people to their chief magistrate.

His personal relation to the throngs was one of joyous comradeship. A crowd of clamorous enthusiastic American citizens drew him irresistibly. At every halt he was met by eager demands for a speech, yet it was manifestly impossible for him to speak everywhere. At first he gave himself up unreservedly to the various committees

which tumbled into his car at every city
and State line, and tried to drag him forth
even before the train had come to a halt.
But experience showed that this was fool-
hardy. In the mad push and crush and
confusion a false start not only hopelessly dislocated the official program, but
endangered life and limb. Major Hunter
of his suite received serious injuries from
mere pressure of the crowd. Lincoln
learned to sit quietly in his car till told
that preparations had been deliberately
completed. But it was easy to see that
this cost him both effort and pain. His
sympathy with the people made him shrink
from any protest against these eager first
greetings; and though his judgment bade
him refuse the popular calls for his presence outside, his heart and feelings were
with the shouting multitude.

At Indianapolis, the first stopping-
place, he struck the key-note of his duty
and theirs in the coming crisis. " The

maintenance of this government," he declared, " is your business, and not mine.
I wish you to remember, now and forever,
that if the Union of these States and the
liberties of this people shall be lost, it is
but little to any one man of fifty-two years
of age, but a great deal to the thirty millions of people who inhabit these United
States and to their posterity in all coming
time. It is your business to rise up and
preserve the Union and liberty for yourselves, and not for me."

This was not the usual complimen-
tary oratory. It was a blast of cool logic,
and had in it a ring of authority. Already
he was the ruler. In Douglas's bullying
tones these words might have sounded like
a threat. But spoken with Lincoln's deep
earnestness, the reasonableness of his position was manifest, and his auditors felt
sure he would aid them to the utmost in
their efforts to preserve the Union for
themselves and their children.

Whenever time would permit, public evening receptions were arranged; but these functions, added to the day's fatigue of travel and official ceremony, were a serious tax upon his strength. His friends urged him to stand where he could bow to the passers-by, instead of shaking hands. The experiment was tried, but he speedily rebelled. It changed live personal contact into meaningless show. He seemed to be on exhibition like some wild animal, and felt separated by an enormous chasm from the people with whom it was his duty, now, more than ever before, to come into close relation. This was worse than any amount of fatigue, and he returned to the old way, where a cordial grasp of the hand, and a fitting word established instantaneous sympathy.

The experiences of the first day developed both the enthusiasm and the difficulties of the journey. A letter written that night told of the crowds. " The house is literally jammed full of people. Three or four ladies and as many gentlemen have even invaded the room assigned to Mr. Lincoln; while outside the door I hear the crowd grumbling and shouting in almost frantic endeavor to get to another parlor at the door of which Mr. Lincoln stands shaking hands with the multitude. It is a severe ordeal for us, increased tenfold for him."

But the letter said nothing about Mr. Lincoln's greatest ordeal that day, which was nothing less than the loss of his inaugural address. It had been written and printed with the utmost secrecy before leaving Springfield; but with curious optimism Mr. Lincoln placed it for the journey in a little old-fashioned black oil-cloth carpet-bag, which he gave in charge of his eldest son, Robert, without telling him what the bag contained.

To Robert, full of the exuberant carelessness of eighteen, the trip seemed much more a triumphal progress than to his father. In the recent campaign he had come in for a certain amount of notice as the " Prince of Rails," a pendant to his father's sobriquet, " The Illinois Rail-Splitter "; and at every stopping-place a group of " the boys " stood ready to seize upon him and do the honors after their own capricious fashion.

At Indianapolis, partly from inexperience on the part of the travelers, partly from insufficient police control, only a portion of the suite reached the carriages intended for them. The rest, including Robert, had to force their way, luggage in hand, as best they could, to their hotel. Even so they reached it long before the others, who were being conscientiously driven through the streets in procession. No sooner had Mr. Lincoln arrived and worked his way through the packed corri-

dors to his room, than he was called out
again, to address the crowd from a bal-
cony.

When at last he had time to think of
the little black bag, Robert was not to
be found. Feverish inquiries developed
that he was off with " the boys," and still
more time elapsed before he could be lo-
cated and brought back. To his father's
impetuous questions he replied with bored
and injured virtue that having arrived in
the confusion, with no room to go to, he
had handed the bag to the hotel clerk —
after the usual manner of travelers.

" And what did the clerk do with it? "
his father asked.

" It is on the floor behind the counter,"
was the complacent answer.

Visions of his inaugural in all the morning papers floated before the President-
elect, as without a word he threw open
his door and began making his way
through the crowded halls to the office.

164

One single stride of his long legs swung him across the clerk's desk, and he fell upon the small mountain of luggage accumulated behind it. Taking a little key from his pocket, he began delving for black bags, and opening such as the key would unlock, while bystanders craned their necks, and the horrified clerk stood open-mouthed. The first half dozen yielded an assortment of undesired and miscellaneous articles; then he came upon his own, inviolate — and Robert had no more porter's duty during the rest of the trip.

It was not the least of the strange contrasts in Mr. Lincoln's career, that after the enthusiasm and acclamations of this journey, he was forced to enter Washington secretly, under cover of night. News of the plot against his life, coming from two sources, equally trustworthy, was too serious to disregard; and though he was averse to such a course, believing that

165

ABRAHAM LINCOLN

" assassination of public officers is not an
American crime," he was too impartial and
just to deny that this was no longer a
question of his personal desires, or even
of his private life, but of the orderly
transmission of authority.

When it became known that the President-elect had entered the Nation's capital
in such manner, great was the wonder
and the criticism. The town was semi-
Southern, and not at all inclined to greet
the newcomer with open arms. This act
gave another peg upon which to hang
criticism. Stanton, with a world of ma-
lignity in his tone, spoke of the way Lincoln "crept into Washington." Others
called it "that smuggling business." No
one seemed to reflect that it required more
courage for a brave man to conquer his
natural aversion to such a course than to
follow his impulse and disregard the warning.

The Presidential party was quartered

at Willard's. " The original plan was to
go to a private house which had been
rented for the occasion," we learn by a
letter from one of the suite. " This plan
having been changed, and no rooms having
been reserved, all the party except Mr.
and Mrs. Lincoln have but sorry accommodations."

Here during the week before inauguration Lincoln received visits of ceremony
from President Buchanan and the outgoing
cabinet, from his rivals in the recent campaign, Douglas and Breckinridge, from
the fruitless Peace Congress then in session, which came in a body, headed by its
chairman, Ex-president Tyler, and from
many lesser social and political lights.
Here also, when such formalities were not
in progress, the crowded hotel parlors,
so thronged " as to make it seem like having a party every night," turned a battery
of not altogether friendly eyes upon the
President-elect and his suite. His sim-

plicity of manner and his apt replies alternately amused and impressed the onlookers.

Douglas especially, critical and a bit malicious, yet full of State pride, and of admiration for Lincoln personally, watched him. " He has not yet got out of Springfield," he said. " He has his wife with him. He does not know that he is President-elect of the United States, sir. He does not see that the shadow he casts is any bigger now than it was last year — but he will soon find it out when he is once inside the White House."

" There is not the slightest apprehension about trouble at the Inauguration — or any other time. That cloud has blown over," one of the suite wrote home. That was the universal hope, yet General Scott saw to it that all possible precautions were taken. Military preceded and followed and trotted in double files on each side of the carriage in which the two Presidents

TO THE COMMITTEE OF ARRANGEMENTS

For the RECEPTION OF THE PRESIDENT ELECT :

GENTLEMEN:—

Being charged with the responsibility of the safe conduct of the President elect, and his suite to their destination, I deem it my duty, for special reasons which you will readily comprehend, to offer the following suggestions :

First: The President elect will under *no circumstances* attempt to pass through any crowd until such arrangements are made as will meet the approval of Col. Ellsworth, who is charged with the responsibility of all matters of this character, and to facilitate this, you will confer a favor by placing Col. Ellsworth in communication with the chief of your escort, immediately upon the arrival of the train.

SECOND: ARRANGEMENT OF CARRIAGES:

FIRST CARRIAGE,

THE PRESIDENT ELECT,
COL. LAMON, or other Members of his Suite,
One or two members of the Escort or Committee.

SECOND CARRIAGE,

COL. E. V. SUMNER, U S. A.,
MAJ. D. HUNTER, U. S. A.,
HON. N. B. JUDD, of Illinois,
HON. DAVID DAVIS, of Illinois,

THIRD CARRIAGE,

COL. E. E. ELLSWORTH,
CAPT. HAZZARD.
JOHN G. NICOLAY, Esq. Private Secretary,
Member of the Escort.

FOURTH CARRIAGE,

ROBT. T. LINCOLN,
JOHN M. HAY, Assistant Secretary,
Two Members of the Escort,

The other members of the suite may be arranged at your pleasure by your committee on the cars. Two carriages will be required to convey Mrs. Lincoln and family and her escort from the cars.

ARRANGEMENT OF ROOMS:

Mr. Lincoln's Secretaries will require rooms contiguous to the President elect.
A private dining room with table for six or eight persons.
Mr. Wood will also require a room near the President elect, for the accommodation of himself and Secretary.
The other members of the suite will be placed as near as convenient.
For the convenience of the committee, a list of the names of the suite arranged in their proper order is appended.
Trusting, gentlemen, that inasmuch as we have a common purpose in this matter, the safety, comfort and convenience of the President elect, these suggestions will be received in the spirit in which they are offered, I have the honor to be your Obedient Servant,

W S. WOOD, Superintendent.

Handbill used on Lincoln's Journey to Washington

rode to the Capitol on the morning of Inauguration. Squads of riflemen were posted on the roofs of commanding houses along Pennsylvania Avenue. Cavalry guarded the side-street crossings along the route of the procession. There were riflemen in the windows of the Capitol; and on the brow of Capitol Hill, in a position to command the approach, and also the broad plaza where the out-door ceremonies took place, a battery of flying artillery stood ready either to thunder forth a salute, or to do more deadly work.

With the mailed hand thus very thinly disguised in the glove of ceremony, Lincoln was made President. Fortunately there was not the slightest disturbance. " A fine day and a fine display. A gratifying and glorious inauguration," was the summing up sent back to Illinois.

The focus of all eyes was a group of four men, representing the political past and future of the country. One of them was Douglas, who had brought about the repeal of the Missouri Compromise. Another was Chief Justice Taney, who had announced the Dred Scott decision. A third was Buchanan, whose use and misuse of official power had helped on the mischief born of these two acts. The fourth was Lincoln, who must now bring the country through the crisis they had done so much to precipitate.

Very strong and vigorous he looked, in contrast with the white-haired, withered Buchanan. Very tall he loomed over the short and stocky Douglas, who courteously held his hat when he rose to deliver his inaugural address. Very clear and far-reaching his voice sounded over the listening crowd as he spoke words which could not be misunderstood.

No President ever entered upon his duties with so impartial yet so firm a declaration of official intention. His inaugural declared the Union perpetual, the Con-

stitution unbroken, ordinances of secession
void. He would maintain the Government
and execute the laws, but there would be
no violence or bloodshed unless forced upon
the National authority. " In your hands,
my dissatisfied fellow countrymen, and
not in mine, is the momentous issue of civil
war." Then, as if this statement of fairness and justice were too harsh, he continued: " I am loath to close. We are
not enemies but friends. We must not be
enemies," and so on to the end of his
appeal for a more perfect understanding.

A cheer greeted the conclusion. Chief
Justice Taney arose, and again Mr. Lincoln looked very tall and vigorous, standing in front of him, as he laid his hand
upon the open Bible and repeated, dis-
tinctly and deliberately, the oath of office.

The battery on the brow of the hill
boomed its salute. Again the people
cheered; and entering their carriage, the
withered old man, and the vigorous

ABRAHAM LINCOLN

Westerner rode back along Pennsylvania
Avenue to the White House, where
Buchanan took cordial leave of the new
President, wishing him success and happi-
ness in his administration.

Success, and happiness!

X

EVERY-DAY LIFE AT THE WHITE HOUSE

THE menace of war, which had been drawing hourly nearer since the election, crossed the threshold by his side. Speaking to an old friend, months later, Lincoln said: " Browning, of all the trials I have had since I came here, none begin to compare with those I had between the inauguration and the fall of Fort Sumter. They were so great that could I have anticipated them, I would not have believed it possible to survive them. The first thing that was handed me after I entered this room when I came from the inauguration, was the letter from Major Anderson, saying that their provisions would be ex-

173

hausted before an expedition could be sent to their relief."

Before the administration was an hour old the issue was upon him, yet the North would talk only of compromise. Horace Greeley had printed an editorial declaring that the Union could not be pinned together with bayonets. Mercantile interests, fearing to lose Southern trade, clamored loudly for concession. Buchanan had apologized to Ex-president Tyler for allowing a few soldiers to carry the flag through the streets of the capital on Washington's birthday. Public opinion was awry. To use Lincoln's own forceful words, " sinners were calling the righteous to repentance." In Washington men protested their loyalty to the new President in the morning, and at night started south to join the confederacy. Congress had adjourned without providing means to meet the rebellion. It fell upon Lincoln, not only to make momentous decisions, but to

assume responsibilities rightly belonging
to the legislative branch of the Government.

For, though the fall of Fort Sumter
cleared the air, and drew the line sharply
between patriotism and treason, it precipitated a flood of new questions — how to
provide troops; how to get money to pay
troops; how to choose efficient generals to
lead troops; and how to answer the questions foreign governments were sure to ask.

Once started, from small beginnings of
riot and panic, and an early harvest of
death which seemed appalling, yet would
have passed unnoticed in the slaughter of
later campaigns, the avalanche of war
swept on through four interminable years.
After the expectation of speedy victory
died away, it was Lincoln's lot to watch
with sickening anxiety the procession of
unsuccessful campaigns, and to learn by
sad experience the deficiencies of his generals.

ABRAHAM LINCOLN

The slow grinding torture of those
days — the thing which wore on him, body
and soul, and turned him from a vigorous
man to an old one, was not the physical
labor of the Presidency, immense as that
was — nor his realization of the horror
and waste of war, deep as that was. It
was seeing the need with such pitilessly
clear vision, grasping the vast problem
with the logic which made him " the ablest
strategist of the war," and yet being unable to infuse his own spirit and vision
into the men through whom the fight must
be made. Even his subordinates felt this.
His secretary longed " to get into the most
active and hottest part of the fight, wherever that may be." " This being where I
can overlook the whole war and never be
in it — always threatened with danger and
never meeting it — constantly worked to
death and yet accomplishing nothing,
grows exceedingly irksome. It is a feel-

176

Please accept my sincere thanks for your kind congratulation.

It affords me pleasure to confirm the confidence you so generously express in the friendly disposition of the United States, through me, towards the Sovereigns, and Governments, you respectively represent— With equal satisfaction I accept the assurances you are pleased to give, that the same disposition is reciprocated by your Sovereigns, your Governments, and Yourselves—

Allow me to express the hope that these friendly relations may remain undisturbed; and also my fervent wishes, for the health and happiness of yourselves personally,—

Autograph Text of Address to Foreign Envoys

ing of duty and not of inclination which keeps me here."

If these were the feelings of the young man who knew he could throw himself into the thick of the fight whenever he chose to leave the post to which he had been assigned, how much more must have been the suffering of his chief, on whom the whole crushing responsibility lay, and whom no earthly power could release. No wonder he said to General Schenck: "If to be the head of Hell is as hard as what I have to undergo here, I could find it in my heart to pity Satan himself."

A memorandum in the handwriting of my father, found in a sealed envelope endorsed, "A private paper, Conversation with the President, October 2, 1861," though the merest skeleton of their talk, shows how uncompromisingly he faced conditions.

ABRAHAM LINCOLN

Fremont ready to rebel.

Chase despairing.

Cameron utterly ignorant and regardless of the course of things, and the probable result. Selfish and openly discourteous to the President. Obnoxious to the country. Incapable either of organizing details or conceiving and executing general plans.

FINANCIAL.

Credit gone at St. Louis.
" Cincinnati.
" Springfield.

Immense claims left for Congress to audit.

Over-draft to-day, Oct. 2, 1861, $12,-000,000.

Chase says new loan will be exhausted in 11 days.

MILITARY.

Kentucky successfully invaded.

Missouri virtually seized.

178

LIFE AT WHITE HOUSE

October here, and instead of having a force
ready to descend the Mississippi, the
probability is that the Army of the West
will be compelled to defend St. Louis.

Testimony of Chase
　　　　　　Bates
　　the　Blairs
　　　　　Meigs
　　　　　Gower
　　　　　Gurley
　　　　　Browning
　　　　　Thomas, that everything in
the West, military and financial, is in
hopeless confusion.

And in view of odds like these it was his
duty to keep up the spirits of the country!
To foster the morale of the people, without
which victories in the field would have been
as impossible as for the soldiers to breathe
without oxygen. The strength and natural buoyancy of the man who could look
such situations in the face, and smile, and
tell stories, is difficult to comprehend.

Once, months after it happened, the President told of being wakened at night at the Soldiers' Home by a general who came in a panic to urge the immediate flight of McClellan's army from Harrison's Landing, the soldiers to be hurried away on transports, and their horses killed, because it was evident they could not be saved. " Thus often," said the President, " I, who am not a specially brave man, have had to restore the sinking courage of these professional fighters in critical times."

But he was only human. His early fits of gloom, conquered and fought down, were occasionally echoed in these moods, when he seemed constrained to think aloud, before a listener he could trust — not for the benefit of the other's advice, but to get his thought into words. Possibly also he craved the listener's silent sympathy. Carl Schurz wrote of such an interview, and Leonard Swett told of being sent for by Lincoln, who read letters from Americans and foreigners about emancipation, and then, laying the letters aside, discussed the question himself from many points of view, without asking Mr. Swett's advice, or even seeking to impress his own ideas upon him. Mr. Swett felt himself more an observer of the President's mental processes than a hearer of his voice. Finally he wished his visitor a safe journey home, and the audience was over. Evidently this earlier talk with his secretary was the outcome of another such imperative need. That it was unusual, and impressive, is plain from the manner in which the note was preserved.

In spite of the war, daily life went on, as daily life must, in a round of incidents trivial in themselves. The tragic background was made endurable by a great hope, and against it details of commonplace living etched a curious, inconsequent, never-ending pattern.

181

Lincoln was servant of the people equally by heart's impulse and in fulfilment of his oath. Every hour was dedicated to their service. His day began early, and ended only when physical weariness drove him to his bed. Frequently at night he could not sleep, and rose to wander from room to room.

At first all his time was taken up with office seekers. " The grounds, halls, stairways, closets, are filled with applicants, who render ingress and egress difficult," Secretary Seward wrote. Mr. Lincoln began by trying to receive these importunates, and attend to official business, twelve full hours a day. Later his reception hours were limited, in theory, from ten o'clock to one; but it was in theory only.

" I am looking forward with a good deal of eagerness to when I shall have time to at least read and write my letters in peace without being haunted continually by some one who ' wants to see the President

182

for only five minutes.' At present this request meets me from almost every man, woman and child I see, whether by day or by night, in the house, or on the street," my father wrote when they had been in Washington three weeks.

That day of leisure never came. Before the office-seekers had been disposed of, war filled the house with a totally different class of visitors — men who wanted commissions, others who wished to furnish stores to the army, inventors with improved engines of destruction, and a never-ending stream of officers in search of promotion.

Although, with the voluntary resignations of officials who went south to join the rebellion, and the countless military appointments made necessary by the new armies, no President has had such an increase in the number of places at his disposal, they were not nearly enough for the hungry hordes. " Gentlemen," he said to a group who urged the benefit of the climate as additional reason for appointing their candidate Commissioner to the Sandwich Islands, " I am sorry to say that there are eight other applicants for the place, all sicker than your man."

That was long before the days of Civil Service reform, but Lincoln's ideas of fairness gave a full equivalent. The patient thoroughness he lavished on his appointments has inspired many reminiscences.

" What is the matter? " a friend asked in alarm, coming upon him sad and depressed. " Have you bad news from the army? "

" No, it is n't the army," he replied with one of his weary, humorous smiles. " It is the post-office at Brownsville, Missouri."

He had steadily refused to make any promises before his election. " I will go to Washington, if at all, an unpledged man," he declared. " Justice to all " was the motto he announced to Mr. Seward when he tendered him the office of Secretary of State, and he steadfastly and consistently tried to enforce it, even down to the post-office at Brownsville, Missouri.

War's toll brought an increasing number of applications for office on the part of disabled soldiers and also of soldiers' widows. " My conclusion is," he wrote the Postmaster General, " that other things being equal, they have the better right."

Justice to all included the Government as well as individuals, and prompted letters like the following:

MY DEAR SIR: I understand a bill is before Congress by your instigation, for taking your office from the control of the Department of the Interior, and considerably enlarging the powers and patronage of your office. The proposed change may be right for aught I know, and it certainly is right for Congress to do as it thinks proper in the case. What I wish to say is, that if the change is made, I do not think I can allow you to retain the office; because that would be encouraging officers to be constantly intriguing, to the detriment of the public interest, in order to profit themselves.

In the rare cases where justice to all could be combined with special favors, he took particular pleasure. Having a specially warm spot in his heart for artists and men of letters, he asked the Secretary of State to " watch out " for " some of those moderate-sized consulates which facilitate artists a little in their profession," in order that he might gratify the sculptor who made his " mud-head," and certain other talented youths, William Dean Howells among them. It is to be observed, however, that he did not direct the Secretary of State to *create* opportunities — he only asked him to watch for them.

One favor which he had no cause to regret he granted with some reluctance.

186

Executive Mansion.
April 11. 1861.

Hon. P. M. G.
   Sir—
      Has a Post-Master been appointed, as yet, at Covington, Ky. Col. Carpenter, wishes John S. Scott to be appointed— He says Scott, is a Douglas Union- man. I know nothing as to the propriety of this; but write to keep a pro= mise.
               Lincoln

The incumbent of this office is a Mr Holt on whose behalf the Hon Mr Holt is interested & applied indirectly to me for his retentions
           M B

President's Note about a Post-office Appointment, with
Montgomery Blair's Endorsement

LIFE AT WHITE HOUSE

It became evident before they left Springfield that my father would need an assistant, and he ventured to ask that his friend, John Hay, be allowed to accompany them. Mr. Lincoln at first demurred: "I can't take all Illinois with me!" he said, with a whimsical grimace.

Occasionally justice and common sense inspired him to benevolent despotism in appointments as in other matters.

"Dear Sir: I personally wish Jacob Freese of New Jersey to be appointed colonel for a colored regiment, and this regardless of whether he can tell the exact shade of Julius Cæsar's hair," was one of the characteristic notes sent to Stanton. It probably made the choleric Secretary of War sputter with wrath, but accomplished its worthy end.

Although Lincoln's manner was one of almost unfailing good humor and quiet tolerance, there were times when he showed that his patience had limits. When the

187

flood of place-seekers was at its height, a
delegation came to urge California appointments which were earnestly opposed
by Lincoln's early friend, Colonel E. D.
Baker, who had become Senator from Oregon. The spokesman of the delegation,
both in his speech and in the papers he
presented, made bitter and criminal accu-
sations against Baker, which the President
knew to be unfounded. He intimated as
much, but the accuser persisted. Lincoln
heard him through in silence, and when he
had finished handed him back the papers.

"Keep them, sir," the man said. "I
wish you to keep them. They are yours."

"Mine to do with as I please?" the
President asked quickly.

"Yes," was the reply.

Mr. Lincoln stepped to the fireplace,
thrust the papers between the blazing
brands, and as the room was lighted by the
fresh flame dismissed the interviewers with
a stern "Good morning, gentlemen."

LIFE AT WHITE HOUSE

One of his wearisome and unavoidable
tasks was signing commissions sent over
every day from the War and Navy Departments. Every appointment and promotion in the regular army, as well as
many in the volunteer service, necessitated
a new commission. These, made out on
heavy parchment, very oily and hard to
write upon, would be placed on his desk in
piles six or eight inches high, and he would
sit working away at them with the patient
industry of a laborer sawing wood.

His correspondence also took much time,
though he read only about one in a hundred of the letters addressed to him. He
rarely dictated. He either made a verbal
or written summary for his secretary, or
carefully wrote out the whole himself —
and frequently carefully copied it. All his
important state papers and political letters
were signed with his full name. His signature on less formal documents was " A. Lincoln." The range of his daily correspond-

ence ran the whole gamut from naming a baby to the most important national and international affairs, and in addition he made many endorsements, some of them lengthy, on communications he did not answer.

" O. H. P. trying to resign an office which he does not hold," was one of them. Another read:

" It seems to me Mr. C. knows nothing about the weather in advance. He told me three days ago that it would not rain again till the thirtieth of April or first of May. It is raining now, and has been for ten hours. I cannot spare any more time to Mr. C." Such notes were apt to express a certain finality.

Among the most beautiful of his letters were those written to parents whose sons had died in battle. " He bore the sorrows of the nation in his heart," as John Hay said. No amount of repetition could dull his ears to the pitiful cry of bereavement.

190

F. S. B. wants to
D. M. Com. or something
of the sort

I think after all, but
am not sure, that he is
a drunken ~~loafer~~,

O. H. P. try-
ing to resign an office
which he does not hold,

Please come to bedroom
½ past ten to-day,

A Lincoln

**Two Characteristic Endorsements, and a Call to a Special
Cabinet Meeting**

LIFE AT WHITE HOUSE

When young Ellsworth, whom he knew personally, was killed at Alexandria, one of the first victims of the war, he not only wrote to his parents, but directed that his body be brought to the White House as if he were his own son; and the funeral was held in the great East Room.

Gradually under the strain of responsibility and care, his demeanor changed. He was just as cordial, just as kindly; but his infectious laughter was less often heard; and from brooding on serious and weighty things he acquired an air of detachment. "Lincoln's prevailing mood in later years was one of meditation," my father wrote. "Unless engaged in conversation, the external world was a thing of minor interest. Not that he was what is called absentminded. He did not forget the spectacles on his nose, and his eye and ear lost no sound or movement about him when he sat writing in his office or passed along the street. But while he

191

noted external incidents, they remained secondary. His mind was ever busy in reflection. Sometimes he would sit for an hour, still as a petrified image, his soul absent in the wide realm of thought." Then the entrance of a friend would summon his spirit back, the kindling eye and quaint remark would anticipate the friendly hand clasp, and wit and practical common sense rule the interview.

Even a President as hard working as Lincoln had to have relaxation. He used to drive late in the afternoon; though this could hardly be called diversion, since his objective point was apt to be one of the earthworks which circled Washington, or one of the military hospitals.

He gave much attention to the hospitals; especially to the building of one which should be a model; consulting the doctor in charge over ingenious devices for the comfort of the wounded, and paying

192

for some of them out of his own pocket. He also provided flower seeds to turn the square in which it stood into something less dismal than a waste of clay and weeds.

In his visits to the hospitals he gave out far more vitality and sympathy than he gained. "There was no medicine equal to the cheerfulness his visit inspired, but its effect on him was saddening in the extreme," said one who watched him on such a round.

His influence upon the well was no less marked than upon the sick. A nineteen-year-old surgeon who was detailed to take Mr. Lincoln through the hospital at City Point just a week before the assassination, never forgot leading him through ward after ward, until finally they came to that filled with sick and wounded prisoners. With a feeling of patriotic duty, he said: "Mr. President, you won't want to go in there; they are only rebels." The President stopped, and laying his large hand on his shoulder gently answered, " You mean Confederates."

Mr. Lincoln had a quick comprehension of mechanical principles, and found both amusement and interest in the cloud of inventors with devices important or visionary, that the war brought to Washington. One proposed to do away with the need for bridges by giving each soldier a pair of little watertight canoes, one for each foot. Another had an epoch-making scheme for moving artillery by means of iron-clad balloons. Some of them obtained permission to set up models in the White House basement, and the grounds south of the Executive Mansion became a favorite place for trying the new guns. When he could escape from the labors of the office, or omit his daily drive, Mr. Lincoln stole away to watch the experiments, to take his turn at the shooting, and enjoy the remarks of the bystanders. He quoted with deep appre-

ciation the verdict of one man, who com-
demned a marvelous gun because of its
slight recoil. " It would not do," he said.
" Too much powder. A good piece of audience should n't rekyle. If it did at all,
it should rekyle a little forrid."

Flag raisings and reviews became as
much a part of the routine as breakfast.
Lincoln's first Fourth of July as President
was marked by both these functions.
" One pretty incident of the review," my
father wrote, " was the passing of the
Garibaldi Guards, a regiment made up entirely of foreigners, whose colonel's com-
mands in French were translated in
process of transmission to the men into
German, Spanish, Italian, Hungarian, and
several other tongues. Each man had
stuck a flower or a sprig of green into his
hat, and as the successive ranks passed the
President, they took them out and threw
them toward him, until he stood in a perfect shower of leaves and blossoms." One

195

wonders what became of these sons of the Old World who paid floral tribute to the Son of the Prairies. They were sent across the Potomac, " and having an idea that there was a fight ahead, marched singing the Marseillaise, with loaves of bread stuck on the points of their bayonets "— and so, out of history.

An ingenuous soldier boy wrote home to his family in Maine that at the flag-raising the President wore plain citizen's clothes " with blue kid gloves " which were short at the wrist and showed his bare arm as he pulled the rope " with as much deliberation as though he had been working his old flatboat down the river."

Sudden emotion choked the boy as the colors floated free, and a burst of military music and cheering filled the air. But it was the President's smile which impressed him most. " I think I should willingly ride fifty miles to vote for him again as I did last November," he wrote.

196

He watched the 71st New York escort Mr. Lincoln back to the White House. "I wish you could have seen him march. He paid little or no attention to the music of Dodworth, but paced off at an irregular rate "— the pioneer gait that he never exchanged for city-bred movements —" while Mr. Seward, whose arm he held, was seen to keep step, his 'left foot on the down beat.' "

The boy lingered near the White House until he saw the President at one of the windows, spyglass in hand, looking toward the Old Dominion. How many times he used that glass to sweep the Virginia hills! How many times he and Mr. Seward traveled the same road, not quite in step, but one in purpose! How many, many times his smile and spirit won men and women as they captivated that boy!

XI

LINCOLN was an unusually affectionate and indulgent father. A
paragraph in a letter to his friend Speed
shows that he and his wife had the experiences and emotions common to proud
parents.

We have another boy, born the 10th of
March. He is very much such a child as
Bob was at his age, rather of a longer order.
Bob is " short and low," and I expect always
will be. He talks very plainly — almost as
plainly as anybody. He is quite smart
enough. I sometimes fear that he is one of
the little rare-ripe sort that are smarter at

about five than ever after. He has a great
deal of that sort of mischief that is the off-
spring of such animal spirits. Since I began
this letter, a messenger came to tell me Bob
was lost; but by the time I reached the house
his mother had found him and had him
whipped, and by now, very likely, he is run
away again.

The second child died in infancy, but
two others were born to them, both boys.
Their father liked to have them with him,
even when to others they appeared decid-
edly troublesome. If they swarmed too
persistently over his person he brushed
them away like gnats, but he never turned
them out of the room or reproved them, except in the mildest manner. When they
began to go to school he studied with
them.

One of his Springfield neighbors, re-
calling how constantly they were in his
company, tells of being attracted to the
door one day by hearing children cry. He

saw Mr. Lincoln striding by with two of his sons, both wailing loudly.

"Why, what is the matter with the boys?" he asked.

"Just what is the matter with the whole world," was the answer. "I've got three walnuts, and each wants two."

"Bob," the eldest, showed a grasp of principles and property rights in dealing with his brothers which foreshadowed success in business and diplomacy. Mr. Lincoln came upon his youngest clinging like a burr to Robert, and demanding a knife the latter held in his hand. "Oh, let him have it, Bob, to keep him quiet," he urged. "No," Bob replied. "It is my knife, and I need it to keep me quiet."

"He promises very well, considering we never controlled him much," the father wrote of this eldest son.

When Lincoln was inaugurated Robert had just entered Harvard. The others, Willie and Thomas, or "Tad," aged ten and eight, respectively, ranged lawless and lovable, over the Executive Mansion. No room was sacred from their intrusion; no conference too weighty to be broken in upon by the rush of their onslaught. They instituted a minstrel show in the attic, and inserted dogs, cats, goats and ponies into various crevices of the domestic establishment.

It was the elder of these, a child of great promise, bright and gentle and studious, who sickened and died in February, 1862. "A fine boy of eleven years, too much idolized by his parents," Attorney-General Bates wrote in his diary; adding that the Government departments were closed on the day of his funeral — the only time, probably, that the death of a child has been so observed in the history of our country.

Lincoln allowed his bereavement to make no difference in his daily tasks, and gave little outward sign of his grief; but his heart lavished its tenderness on his youngest child, Tad, a merry warm-hearted little lad, who interrupted his father's gravest labors with impunity, and found safe refuge in his office from the domestic authorities.

He must have been a winning small boy, in spite of his talent for keeping himself and others in hot water, for even the gruff Secretary of War succumbed, and in a moment of indiscretion commissioned him a lieutenant. Tad's next exploit was to drill the household servants, and one night, to relieve the regular sentries, and put them all on duty. His father, thinking it a good joke, refused to interfere, until the small officer, wearied by his authority, fell asleep, when the Commander-in-Chief of the Army carried him tenderly to bed, and then went downstairs and dismissed the awkward squad.

The boy, running in and out among the

visitors waiting to see the President, became their active champion. One day he rushed into his father's office and asked permission to introduce some " friends," returning with a delegation Mr. Lincoln had been dexterously avoiding. Once inside the door, he stopped, asked the name of the oldest of the group, presented him to his father, and added, " Now, Judge, you introduce the rest! " The President, fairly caught, took him on his knee, kissed him, told him he had introduced his friends like a gentleman, and made the best of an interview which could not be satisfactory to either side.

Lincoln's love for children did not stop with his own sons. He was greeted with ecstasy by the group of grandchildren who roamed over the country place of F. P. Blair, Sr., a few miles from Washington; and they remember to this day the abandon with which he entered into their games, how long his strides were, and how far his coat tails sailed out behind him as he ran.

When children came to him on business in the Executive Office, as they sometimes did, he listened to them with the same courtesy accorded their elders, never denying their requests on account of their youth. Those who criticized the President's merciful unwillingness to impose the death penalty, dreaded to see a woman with a child in her arms enter that room. They knew she would have a speedy and sympathetic hearing. " It was the baby that did it, madam," Edward, the colored usher, observed to one wife who passed out, radiantly tearful.

Mrs. Lincoln was a Kentuckian, and the fact that some of her relatives fought in the Southern armies was enough to keep gossip busy with rumors of her tacit if not open sympathy with the rebellion — gossip which did her grievous wrong, and

204

added one more to the daily trials of the President. It was a thing of which he could take no public notice; but at one time he felt constrained to tell several members of the cabinet his side of the story then current. " He gave the details with frankness and without disguise. . . . They did him credit on a subject of scandal and abuse," one of them wrote.

The President's attitude toward his wife had something of the paternal in it, almost as though she were a child, under his protection. It is said that when President Taylor offered to make him Governor of Oregon Territory, shortly after the end of his term in Congress, Lincoln's refusal was largely because of her unwillingness to go so far into the wilderness.

Personally he was singularly indifferent to physical surroundings, and neither the wilderness, had they gone there, nor the stately proportions and practical inconvenience of the Executive Mansion when they actually experienced them, affected him in the least. But, like many another good American husband, it pleased him to see his wife enjoying luxury; and in March, 1861, the White House must have seemed to both of them a very grand home indeed.

During the war, as for many years after, the President's family and the business of state were housed in uncongenial intimacy. The family lived upstairs in the western end of the building, the offices were in the east end; the state apartments were below; and visitors and office-seekers blocked anterooms and halls; while Tad split the ears of cabinet ministers and long-suffering clerks, as, with mischief and drum, he did what he could to convert this " dwelling-place but not a habitation," into a real home.

The Lincolns were the Western-most people who had inhabited the White House, and were as new to official ceremony as to

I wish Mr Nicolay would invite the following gentlemen to tea at my house, at 5 P.M. tomorrow.

✓ *Mr. Schenck*
✓ *Mr. Pratt*
✓ *Mr. Cartter*
  Mr. Ogden
✓ *Mr. Philips*
✓ *Mr. Hatch*
✓ *Mr. Dubois*
✓ *Mr. Nicolay — himself —*

Saturday, Nov. 3.

                      Lincoln

A Presidential Tea Party

stately surroundings. The President, however, had his native dignity and his term in
Congress to fall back upon; while Mrs.
Lincoln had her woman's wits and that ease
in fitting into more luxurious surroundings
which is the birthright of every living creature, from protoplasm to potentate.

On request the State Department furnished elaborate lists of officials and functions, along with certain helpful details.
From that source or elsewhere they were
advised never to say " Sir " to a titled
foreigner; and that " at evening calls of
diplomats it is well for the President to go
down." The hour for state dinners was
set sternly at seven. The family might
dine at six. A memorandum prescribed
" dress for gentlemen " as " coat, black
dress, or ditto blue with bright buttons —
(never wear frocks)"— which seems to
press the Lincoln régime back into remote
picturesqueness.

With these hints, and their natural good

sense, they got on as well as most new administrations. One of the hints was that "parties, if given, must be entirely informal or accidental." After Mrs. Lincoln had been installed about a year she determined to ignore this rule, and sent out invitations for a party which was not at all "accidental." Society was rocked to its center, and the local papers printed columns detailing the elegance of everybody's manners and costumes, not forgetting the foreigners who must never be addressed as "Sir," and ending with an inventory of the sugar ornaments on the supper table.

Notes made in the house were less saccharine. "Half the city is jubilant at being invited, while the other half is furious at being left out in the cold. It was a very respectable, if not brilliant success. Many of the invited guests did not come, so the rooms were not at all overcrowded. . . . Those who were here (some of them having sought and almost begged their invitations) will be forever happy in the recollection. . . . Suffice it to say that the East Room looked very beautiful; that the supper was magnificent, and that when all was over, by way of an interesting little finale, a couple of the servants, much moved by wrath and wine, had a jolly little knock-down in the kitchen, damaging in its effects to sundry heads and champagne bottles. This last item is strictly *entre nous.*"

That was the culmination of Mrs. Lincoln's social achievements. The very next of these confidential letters, enclosing a newspaper account of the great party, adds: " Since then one of the President's little boys has been so sick as to absorb all his attention." From that time on private and public sorrow put an end to all except the formal and official entertaining.

The traditional state dinners and receptions took place; and there was music in the summer on the White House lawn;

when occasionally the noise of heavy guns
would draw the crowd away from the band
down to the river's edge to gaze across at
the Virginia hills.

The great public receptions were not
disagreeable to the President, and he
seemed surprised when people commiserated
him upon having to endure them. He
would shake hands with thousands of people, seemingly unconscious of what he was
doing, murmuring some monotonous salu-
tation, his eye dim and thoughts far away,
until a familiar face, or the sight of a little child would focus his attention.
" Hurrah for Mist' Linthon!" a small citizen lisped as he came up, convoyed by
his proud parent. " Hurrah for Mister
You!" the President responded, gathering
him in his arms, and giving him a mighty
toss toward the ceiling.

Many people came primed with a speech
to deliver, but unless it was compressed into
the smallest possible space, it never got ut-

terance. If it were brief enough, and caught the President's fancy, it received a swift answer. One night an elderly gentleman from Buffalo said, " Up our way we believe in God and Abraham Lincoln."

" My friend, you are more than half right! " was the President's reply as he passed him on to the next in line.

Lincoln had grown to manhood and prominence in a period of grave formality of manner, in a locality where old Southern traditions of good breeding prevailed. Dignity was as natural to him as honest living or straight thinking. In his audiences with diplomats he lost nothing in comparison with men trained in European courts. His natural poise and sense of fitness made both words and bearing unembarrassed. Yet after complying with all the requirements of custom, his kindly wit was apt to find outlet. When Lord Lyons went to the White House to announce the marriage of the Prince of Wales, he made the customary formal speech. The President answered in like manner; then, taking the bachelor diplomat by the hand, he supplemented it with a genial, " And now, Lord Lyons, go thou and do likewise! "

Contrary to popular belief nobody presumed to call Lincoln " Abe," or had, since he was a boy. " Honest Old Abe " was indeed an expression country-wide, but it was used in speaking about him, not to him. There was that in his bearing, friendly as it was, which forbade familiarity. His own son has told the writer that even his mother addressed her husband as " Mr. Lincoln." Sometimes in talking to men much younger than himself, he called them by their first names, but with those of his own generation, even intimates of his early years, his nearest approach to familiarity was in dropping the prefix " Mr." In this he followed the well-established custom of the time and place.

He was as temperate in his speech as in

his appetites.   His innate honesty forbade
his saying things he did not mean, while
his appreciation of the value of words
made him differentiate between their use
and abuse as he would between the use and
abuse of gold.   He was generous, but no
spendthrift with either.   His hearty " I
am glad to see you," accompanied by a
warm handclasp and his smile, meant more
than another man's extravagant compli-
ments.   If he was not glad he did not say
so.   " Good morning," or " What can I
do for you? " or some equally unperjured
greeting sufficed.   This strict truthfulness
in little things gives added point to his occasional vivid statements; like that to Mr.
Browning about the first weeks of his administration, or his remark to General
Schenck that he could find it in his heart to
pity Satan himself.

With his wealth of sympathy, his conscience, and his unflinching sense of justice, he was predestined to sorrow.   There

was in his nature a strain of deep melancholy, a trait not uncommon among the
pioneers. In his youth, during the years
when blood pounds fastest, and desires and
aspiration protest loudest against the stern
discipline of fact, it came upon him time
and again; and because he was different
from his fellows — a finer instrument, re-
sponding more readily to calls of the spirit
— it hurt cruelly. "If what I feel were
equally distributed to the whole human
family, there would not be one cheerful face
on the earth." From one so temperate in
speech, these words mean much.

By the time he reached middle life the
sharpness of these attacks had been lived
down, but a melancholy underlay all his
moods — even his merriest. He was still
vibrant to chords of feeling.

"I believe I feel trouble in the air before
it comes," he said, entering the room of his
secretaries to bring news of a military dis-
aster which had just reached him.

HIS WIFE AND CHILDREN

"I am superstitious," he admitted frequently, but in the next breath was apt to give a good and sensible reason for what he was pleased to call his superstition. He placed enough importance on dreams to tell them; not only his recurrent dream of the ship and the dark shore, but others. Once he sent a despatch to his wife, advising her to put away Tad's pistol, because he had had " an ugly dream " about him.

In unguarded moments he gave way to grief with complete unconsciousness. The gray, drawn look of his face in mental pain; his " ghostlike " appearance as he walked up and down the room, exclaiming, " My God, my God! what will the country say?"; the way the tears ran unheeded down his cheeks while he inspected the *Monitor* and lived again in imagination that memorable battle; his stumbling steps and hands pressed to his heart as he went from McClellan's headquarters, heedless of the sentinel's salute, on learning of Col-

215

ABRAHAM LINCOLN

onel Baker's death — betrayed how completely he forgot himself in grief.

Fortunately his joy was as spontaneous as a child's. No amount of experience made him callous to either happiness or pain. " I myself will telegraph the news to General Meade! " he cried, seizing his hat when Secretary Welles brought word that Vicksburg had fallen. Then he stopped, his face beaming, caught Welles's hand and almost embracing him cried, " What can we do for the Secretary of the Navy for this glorious intelligence? He is always giving us good news. I cannot tell you my joy over the result. It is great, Mr. Welles, it is great! "

Yet such was his self-control that he could make his face a mask when he saw fit, and it was not often that casual visitors realized the depth of his feeling. One secret of his success had been his power of inspiring confidence in his followers. One duty of his high office he felt to be keeping
216

up the spirits of his countrymen during the dark hours of war. He had need of his great physical endurance, and all his self-control. Many were the sleepless nights he passed after that first Sunday when he remained in his office until dawn, listening to the excited tales of those who had witnessed sights and sounds of the battle of Bull Run.

His was the faith which moves mountains. He could even extract a bitter comfort from sad news. Being told of heavy firing in the direction of Knoxville, at a time when he was very anxious, he said that anything which showed that General Burnside was not overwhelmed, was cheering. "Like Sallie Carter, when she heard one of her children cry, he could say, 'there goes one of my young ones, not dead yet, bless the Lord!'"

He wore his greatness so naturally that he could afford to jest. Living by the same rule in matters great and small,

ABRAHAM LINCOLN

whether signing an emancipation proclamation or attending to the trifling demands
of a child, he did not have to put on added
solemnity for great occasions, and he gathered what comfort and relief he could from
the flickering bits of humor that crossed
his path.

Although wanting in the language of
gallantry, he was not incapable of turning
a neat compliment.   The artist Carpenter
has told of one which would have pressed
Chesterfield hard.   An enthusiastic lady
gave the President an entirely superfluous
bouquet.   The situation was momentarily
embarrassing, but " with no appearance
of discomposure, he stooped down, took
the flowers, and looking from them into the
sparkling eyes and radiant face of the
lady, said, with a gallantry I was unpre-
pared for, ' Really, madam, if you give
them to *me*, and they are *mine*, I think I
cannot possibly make so good a *use* of them
as to present them to *you* in return ! ' "

HIS WIFE AND CHILDREN

He was the most abstemious of men. Not that he remained on principle a total abstainer as he was during part of his early life; but he never cared for wines or liquors of any sort, and never used tobacco. Judge Lawrence Weldon once overheard Douglas trying to ridicule him on this point.

"What! You a temperance man?" Douglas asked.

"No," drawled Lincoln, with a smile. "I'm not a temperance man; but I'm temperate in this — to wit — I don't drink."

At table he ate sparingly, without seeming to know what he was eating. When Mrs. Lincoln was away he sometimes absentmindedly omitted the formality of dining altogether. To some visitors who apologized for sending in their cards at the dinner hour, he replied:

"It makes no difference. When my wife is away I just browse around."

219

It was the company, not the meat,
which interested him. Carl Schurz, for
whom he had a strong liking, once asked
leave to present his German brother-in-
law, a young merchant from Hamburg.
Mr. Lincoln told him to bring him the next
day about lunch time, adding casually that
there would be something to eat. Schurz
had no little difficulty in quieting his
guest's trepidation. His assertion that
there would be no court etiquette or formality whatever was too wild for the foreigner's belief. When he found himself
greeted like an old friend, and the three
sat down alone to luncheon, he pulled himself out of his stupefaction, and answered
entertainingly the many questions about
Hamburg with which his host plied him.
The meal ended in anecdotes and laughter;
and as they left the White House the
young German was vainly trying to find
words in which to express his puzzled admiration for the man who had risen from

peasant to ruler, and, with so much dignity, remained so unconscious of self.

To his two secretaries he was the embodiment of kindness and friendliness. For a time they occupied a room in the Executive Mansion, and saw him, literally, day and night. Like boys, they had their own names for him. " The Tycoon " was their favorite, with " The Ancient " a close second. When their admiration passed all bounds they gave him the comprehensive title, " The American."

" What a man it is," wrote John Hay in his diary, after detailing a nocturnal visit of the President, who came with a volume of Hood in his hand, to read them something which struck his fancy. " Occupied all day with matters of vast moment, deeply anxious about the fate of the greatest army in the world, with his own fame and fortune hanging on the events of the passing hour, he has such wealth of simple *bonhomie* and good fellowship that

he gets out of bed and perambulates the
house in his shirt to find us that we may
share with him the fun of poor Hood's little conceits."

Personally Lincoln was very brave.
When he visited the army at the front and
reviewed the troops, he was the cause of
much anxiety to the commanders, because
his tall figure, made taller still by the
" stove-pipe " hat he habitually wore, rendered him a conspicuous and unmistakable
target for the enemy. When General
Early's troops came within a few miles of
Washington he was actually under fire at
Fort Stevens, so interested in watching de-
velopments that he was quite impatient at
being made to leave his exposed position.
General Butler confessed that no one ever
gave him a fright equal to Lincoln, because of his calm disregard for personal
safety.

" The Commander-in-Chief of the Army
must n't show any cowardice in the pres-

ence of his soldiers, however he may feel,"
was his laughing reply.

But no instance of his complete forget-
fulness of danger equals his entry into
Richmond, when he walked for two miles
or more, practically unescorted, through
streets of silent houses behind whose closed
blinds despairing women and sad-eyed men
looked on the joy-crazed negroes who surrounded him, calling down blessings upon
his head with all the fervent picturesqueness of their race.

Lincoln's ceremonious uncovering in answer to the sweeping obeisance of a bent
and grizzled negro whose twisted limbs
and white hairs betokened the labors and
injustice heaped upon the race, is one
of the most impressive and dramatic incidents of the war. But to the white onlookers in the houses, inflamed by passion
and made bitter by defeat, it must have
borne a different aspect. A bullet might
very easily have sped from behind one of

those forbidding shutters. To the honor of Richmond, if the temptation came, it was thrust aside, and the Commander-in-Chief of its conquering host passed in safety into the house lately occupied by the President of the Confederacy.

The reverie into which he fell as he rested in Jefferson Davis's own chair was so serious and so deep that the aide on duty did not dare address him. When General Weitzel, in command of the conquered city, reported, and together the two passed through the burned and devastated portions of the town to Libby Prison and Castle Thunder, where memory would have its way, the general turned to him and asked what he was to do about the conquered people.

Lincoln's reply was that he did not wish to give orders upon that subject. " But," he said, in his kindly way, " if I were in your place, I 'd let 'em up easy. Let 'em up easy."

Walt Whitman,. seeing the President drive by seated beside his wife, his carriage drawn by " only two horses, and they nothing extra," thought Lincoln a very ordinary-looking man. He probably thought so himself, but it is doubtful if he was as indifferent to his personal appearance as we have been led to suppose. There were too many passing references in his speeches and in conversation, to warrant the belief that he gave it no thought. One or more of his stories refer to it; he spoke of it at least twice in his debates with Douglas; he said to Mr. Chittenden that though he " did not set up for a beauty " he thought the people of the South would not find him so ugly or so black as he had been painted. He told John Hay of his dream in which a party of plain people began to comment on his appearance, saying he was a very common-looking man, to which he replied, " the Lord prefers common-looking people, that is the reason he makes so many of them." His shuddering comment on a portrait of himself was that it was " horribly like." And there is the final bit of evidence that he took the advice of a little girl, a total stranger, who wrote to him during the campaign, suggesting with childish candor that he would look better if he wore whiskers.

We know that he was proud of, or at least interested in, his great height, and took a boyish delight in measuring himself with any exceptionally tall man he met — to the astonishment, and sometimes to the deep embarrassment of the latter; and that when he had a chance to exhibit his strength of arm — how far he could throw, or how clean and deep a cut he could make with an ax — he seized the opportunity, and showed an ingenuous pride in the excellence of his performance.

The probability is that he was fully aware of the worst aspect of his personal appearance, and regretted it; and had no notion of its best. He was a huge spare man, slightly stooping, who walked with the peculiar slow woods-and-fields movement of the Western pioneer; and who sat, as tall people have to sit, on chairs made for shorter folk, not erect, but disposing of their long limbs as best they may. A sculptor who made most careful measurements and studies from photographs, tells us that, from a sculptor's point of view, Lincoln's proportions were quite perfect. So much for the frame. It was the indwelling spirit which transformed it and baffled description. When sitting withdrawn and musing, one saw only a sad sallow man, on whom the clothes hung loosely. In the glow and excitement of public speaking he was singularly handsome — at times seemed almost inspired. When he looked into the eyes of a fellow being in trouble, he had the most tenderly sympathetic face in the world.

My father strongly denied that Lincoln

227

was careless in his dress. He said that Lincoln's clothes were always scrupulously neat, and were in accord with his means and his surroundings. Reminiscences of the period before his Presidency describe him as wearing a short-waisted black dress coat, and trousers not too long. The West was even less rigid and progressive than the East in matters of costume, and at that period we were not yet far away from the days when the cut of coat which is now a badge of servitude before six P. M. and of emancipation after that hour, was the conservative garment by daylight for all men free, white, and over twenty-one.

The gentleman who met Mr. Lincoln when he went to deliver the Cooper Institute speech tells how he accompanied him to his room at the hotel, and saw him open his grip-sack and shake out a new suit of black broadcloth, which though carefully packed, had become a mass of wrinkles. He hung it up, trusting optimistically that

228

the creases would disappear before he had to put it on. There is something rather pathetic in the picture of this great man doing his inadequate best to appear suitably clad before his Eastern audience. The idea of sending his suit to be pressed never crossed his mind. That was not the way things were managed in his simple household.

He never forgot the dignity of his office, but he could not take its pomp and ceremony seriously. That it could be expected to interfere with his simple and unaffected demeanor as an individual, he refused to admit. He wished to be free to come and go as he chose. His axiom that " he who would be no slave must consent to have no slave " applied in his own mind, as truly to himself as to mankind in the abstract. His propensity for roaming about Lafayette Square, or between the old War Department and the White House, late at night, alone, or accompanied only by one of his secretaries, filled those who knew of the habit with dismay. He admitted that he ran a certain risk of assassination, but contended that the only way to guard against that effectively, was to shut himself up in an iron box, where he could not possibly perform the duties of President. Any measure short of that seemed to him useless. "Why put up the bars," he said, "when the fence is down all around?"

The Secretary of War proposed that the Adjutant-General be detailed to attend him. He answered with characteristic courtesy and decision:

MY DEAR SIR: On reflection I think it will not do, as a rule, for the Adjutant-General to attend me wherever I go; not that I have any objection to his presence, but that it would be an uncompensating encumbrance both to him and to me. When it shall occur to me to go anywhere, I wish to be free to go at once, and not to have to notify the Adjutant-General and wait till he can get ready.

It is better, too, for the public service that he shall give his time to the business of his office, and not to personal attendance on me. While I thank you for the kindness of the suggestion, my view of the matter is as I have stated.

When it was finally decided that a guard must be maintained at the White House, and an escort of cavalry must accompany him on his daily drive, he submitted, though not without humorous protest.

"Why, Mrs. Lincoln and I cannot hear ourselves talk for the clatter of their sabers and spurs; and some of them appear to be new hands and very awkward, so that I am more afraid of being shot by the accidental discharge of a carbine or revolver, than of any attempt upon my life by a roving squad of 'Jeb' Stuart's cavalry."

A guard was, however, only a common precaution, especially during the summer months, when Lincoln rode or drove out through wooded roads to spend the nights at the Soldiers' Home, returning to the Executive Mansion in the early morning. He acknowledged this, and then proceeded with his usual artless democracy to turn official etiquette topsy-turvy by haling General Meade out of the War Department to be presented to the obscure captain of his new guard, on the simple ground that both were from Pennsylvania. Stanton and the rest might post guards all around the lot, but no power on earth could prevent his treating them like men and brothers.

He invited the captain to share his early and frugal breakfast, and the captain thought him the kindest and pleasantest gentlemen he ever met. " He never spoke unkindly of any one, and always spoke of the rebels as ' those Southern gentlemen.' "

The captain used to knock at his door at half past six or seven in the morning, and usually found him reading, though sometimes still busy with his toilet. " All

right.   Just wait a moment, while I repair
damages," he called one morning, when
caught in the act of sewing on a " vital
button."

As a stickler for official ceremony Lincoln was really hopeless. He took most
unpardonable liberties with established
custom, and disconcerting short cuts to results.   Not only would he sew on his own
buttons, or bring a general downstairs to
be introduced to a captain if he chose;
but more than once, in his anxiety to
get first-hand and correct information in
the military and diplomatic service, he invited subordinates to report directly to him
instead of through regular official channels.
No wonder men whose minds worked only
inside a binding of red tape were scandalized.

XII

L INCOLN took his Presidential rivals
into his cabinet, and compelled them
to be his friends; but even his genial soul
could not warm them toward each other.
Seward and Chase were antagonistic.
Stanton and Welles were not in accord.
Cameron, Lincoln's first Secretary of War,
proved insubordinate. Seward meddled
with the Navy and the Law, according to
the heads of those Departments. Bates
had little patience with Stanton. Welles
thought Chase's financial policy all wrong.
Blair seemed to all of them aggressively
mindful of family interests. And each began by believing it his moral duty to help

234

neutralize the great national blunder which had elected Lincoln by guiding and directing him with all the brains at his command.

It could not be called a harmonious company, yet the earnest patriotism in the heart of each, and Lincoln's elastic good nature, held them together fairly well. Newspapers printed sensational accounts of quarrels, and rumors of wholesale cabinet changes; but they continued to work together for the country's good, and changes, when they occurred, were neither wholesale nor sensational.

Lincoln dominated them from the first, though it was long before they found it out. As late as January, 1862, Attorney-General Bates wrote in his diary:

"There is no quarrel among us, but an absolute want of continuity of intelligence, purpose and action. In truth, it is not an administration, but the separate and disjointed action of seven independent officers, each one ignorant of what his colleagues are doing. . . . The President is an excellent man, and in the main wise, but he lacks will and purpose, and I greatly fear he has not the power to command."

Yet even before they were actually his advisers he began his sway. Two days before the inauguration, Seward, suspecting an undue leaning toward the more radical element in the party, attempted to withdraw. Lincoln waited until the inaugural procession was forming in the street, and then sent him a short note, refusing to release him, remarking as he handed it to his private secretary to be copied:

" I cannot afford to let Seward take the first trick."

In Lincoln's mind their mutual relations were clear. The cabinet was not a regency, but a board of advisers. Questions of administration he settled with each department separately. Questions of policy he discussed with his cabinet; but he rarely

asked their vote; and on several occasions
his final decision was against their almost
unanimous judgment. Yet he was patient
to hear advice, and candid to admit the
force of argument. When he had to give
a decision adverse to the majority, he gave
it, not with the pride of authority, but as
though constrained by public duty.

Lincoln's modification of Seward's despatches at the time of the Trent affair,
and his magnanimous handling of that gentleman when in a moment of madness Seward intimated that Lincoln was a failure
as President, offered to do his thinking for
him, and proposed to end the budding rebellion by bringing on war with most of
the military powers of Europe, is an old
story. It is easy to imagine the frigid
note with which Washington would have
dismissed such a minister, or the impetuos-
ity with which Jackson would have thundered him out of his cabinet. Lincoln
answered in a few quiet words, entirely de-

void of passion, pointing out that it was for him and no one else to make final decisions, adding, " I wish, and suppose I am entitled to have, the advice of all my cabinet." Seward was great enough to comprehend his generosity, and so far as is known, the matter was never alluded to between them.

When Secretary Cameron sent out a report in favor of arming negroes for military service, which he knew was at that time contrary to Lincoln's policy, Lincoln showed no anger. He merely recalled the advance copies and asked him to modify the order. For a time the incident seemed forgotten, but one day Cameron was made Minister to Russia, and there was a new Secretary of War.

It is said that on the death of Cardinal Mazarin Louis XIV called his cabinet together and told them that for the future he intended to be his own prime minister. Lincoln made no unnecessary statements, but gradually it dawned upon the cabinet that he was master. Seward was the first to find it out. " There is but one vote in the cabinet, and that is cast by the President," he wrote some weeks after his unbelievable Memorandum of April 1, 1861.

This Westerner whom they had thought to rule had a kingly way of his own. For all his simple manners he gave orders like one born to power. " You will hear all they may choose to say, and report it to me. You will not assume to definitely consummate anything," he instructed Seward when the latter went to meet the commissioners of the Confederacy at Hampton Roads. And when the war was nearing its close he sent word to Grant: " You are not to decide, discuss, or confer upon any political question. Such questions the President holds in his own hands, and will submit them to no military conferences or conventions. Meanwhile you are to press to the utmost your military advantages."

When he read his cabinet the preliminary Proclamation of Emancipation, he told them flatly that he had resolved upon the step, and had not called them together to ask their advice.

No descendant of a hundred kings could be more sure of his right to command. Even Louis could not have been more dictatorial or emphatic; but his methods were characteristically his own.

In 1864 when intrigues within the cabinet reached a pitch that he could no longer ignore, he read his assembled advisers the following impressive little lecture:

" I must myself be the judge how long to retain in, and when to remove any of you from, his position. It would greatly pain me to discover any of you endeavoring to procure another's removal, or in any way to prejudice him before the public. Such endeavor would be a wrong to me; and much worse, a wrong to the country. My wish is that on this subject, no remark be made, nor question asked, by any of

you, here or elsewhere, now or hereafter."

At another time an intrigue set on foot by some friends of Chase, resulted in such criticism of Seward by Republican senators that Seward sent the President his resignation. Lincoln called the censorious senators, and all of the cabinet, except Seward, to a meeting at the White House, neither side knowing that the other was to be present. In the unexpected face-to-face council a very warm discussion took place, and Chase found himself, with the rest of the cabinet, defending Seward. To save his consistency he next day brought the President his own resignation, which was accepted with unflattering alacrity.

A moment later a friend entering the room found Mr. Lincoln alone, regarding the paper with an indescribably whimsical expression.

"Now I can ride," he said. "I have a pumpkin in each end of my bag;" and

ABRAHAM LINCOLN

forthwith sat down and wrote identical
notes to Seward and Chase, asking them
to withdraw their resignations.

Lincoln was well satisfied with this day's
work, by which he had made the critics
thrash out their differences in his presence,
and had saved the services of both his able
ministers to the country. " I do not see
how it could have been done better," he
said. " I am sure it was right. If I had
yielded to that storm and dismissed Seward
the thing would all have slumped over one
way, and we should have been left with a
scanty handful of supporters. When
Chase sent in his resignation I saw the
game was in my own hands, and I put it
through."

The cabinet sessions were absolutely informal. Regular meetings were held at
noon on Tuesdays and Fridays. When
special meetings were necessary the President or Secretary of State called the members together. There was a long table in

the cabinet room, but it was not used as a council board. The President generally stood up and walked about. The others came in and took their seats according to convenience, staying through the session, or stating their business and departing, as pressure of work demanded. Sometimes the meeting was opened by a remark or an anecdote by the President; oftener by the relation of some official or personal happening to one of his advisers.

The many stories of strained relations between Lincoln and Stanton are capable of a gentler interpretation than is usually given them. Stanton was undoubtedly prejudiced against Lincoln in the beginning. This was perhaps the result of an unquiet conscience, since he had treated Mr. Lincoln with scant courtesy in the McCormick Reaper case some years before.

Simon Cameron told my father that when he was made Minister to Russia Lincoln asked whom he wished for his successor in the War Department.   He answered, " Stanton."

" Well," said Lincoln, " go and ask Stanton whether he will take it."

On his way Mr. Cameron met Secretary Chase, and told his errand.   Chase, who had a weakness for feeling that he was pulling the strings and making the puppets dance, said, " Don't go to Stanton's office.   Come with me to my office, and send for Stanton to come there, and we will talk it over together."   They did so, and Stanton agreed to accept the post, possibly in the same spirit of hostile patriotism with which he had entered on his duties under Buchanan.   But there was a rugged honesty in him which could not fail to respond to Lincoln's qualities.   He was as impetuous and explosive as the President was slow to anger; but his bluster was a habit of speech quite as much as a state of mind, and Lincoln bore no malice.

" Did Stanton say I was a d—d fool? "
Lincoln asked when Mr. Lovejoy came in
bewildered rage to report an interview the
President had authorized him to hold with
his Secretary of War.

" He did, sir! "

The President bent his head, then looked
up with his winning smile and remarked,
" If Stanton says I am a d—d fool, I must
be one, for he is nearly always right. I
will slip over and see him." The point of
this and similar stories is that Lincoln
kept his temper, refused to air family differences, official or personal, in public,
and that after " slipping over to see him,"
the matter was arranged.

" This woman, dear Stanton, is a little
smarter than she looks to be "— that message and even his note about Julius
Cæsar's hair, are not the kind a man sends
where relations are seriously strained.

Several members of the cabinet were afflicted with undue seriousness. When the

245

President endorsed a paper, " Referred to
Mars and Neptune," the heads of the War
and Navy Departments looked askance.
When they heard him laugh only a
moment before turning to consider the
weighty matter of the Emancipation Proclamation, they felt that something was
radically wrong. They could scarcely
condone Lincoln's joking; and when Stanton tried to be mildly funny they instantly
scented a scandal. Secretary Welles con-
fided to his diary: " The President still
remains with the army . . . Stanton . . .
remarked that it was quite pleasant to
have the President away. That he
(Stanton) was much less annoyed.
Neither Seward nor myself responded."

Lincoln's remark that he " had n't much
influence with this administration," and
that he was " only the lead-horse who
must n't kick over the traces," was his
way of saying that if he delegated powers
and duties to his cabinet ministers, it was

only fair to refrain from interfering while
they carried them out. "It is a good
thing for individuals that there is a Government to shove over their acts upon.
No man's shoulders are broad enough to
bear what must be," he said; and to critics
of the administration he would answer:

"Suppose all you owned was in gold,
and the gold had been put into the hands
of Blondin to carry across the Niagara
River on a rope — would you shake the
rope and keep shouting contradictory advice; or would you hold your breath and
your tongue, and keep hands off until he
was safely over? The Government is
carrying an immense load and doing the
best it can. Don't badger us. We 'll get
you safe across."

He never lost his sense of proportion.
He used to tell a story of a pilot on a
Western river, who was using every bit of
his skill and vigilance to keep the boat in
the narrow channel, when he felt a tug at

his coat, and heard a boy cry, " Say, Mr. Captain, say! I wish you 'd stop your boat a minute, I 've lost my apple overboard." And he had another story about a steamboat with a " five-foot boiler and a seven-foot whistle " which had to stop stock-still every time the engineer blew a blast.

Criticism which took no more account of values worried him little. " I 'll do the very best I can," he said — " the very best I know how. And I mean to keep doing so till the end. If the end brings me out all right what is said against me won't amount to anything. If the end brings me out wrong, ten angels swearing I was right would make no difference."

Senators seemed to consider themselves specially privileged in the line of criticism.

" I fear I have made Senator Wade my enemy for life," he said ruefully one day. " He was here just now, urging me to dismiss Grant, and in response to something

he said I answered, ' Senator, that reminds
me of a story.' He said in a petulant way,
' It is with you all story, story! You are
letting this country go to hell with your
stories, sir! You are not more than a mile
away from it this minute.' "

" What did you answer? "

" I asked good-naturedly if that was
not just about the distance from here to
the Senate Chamber. He was very angry,
grabbed up his hat and went off."

It is said that the aptness of the retort
worked its way through the senator's anger
before he reached that place " a mile
away," and that he turned back to apolo-
gize. The President's callers were not
always so reasonable; and he was sin-
cerely distressed if any one left him in ill
humor.

With Senator Sumner his relations were
outwardly most cordial, though he was not
insensible to the spirit of criticism which
underlay the smiling intercourse. " I

have never had much to do with bishops,"
he said once, " but, do you know — Sumner is my idea of a bishop."

Sumner was troubled by what he called
" the slow working of Lincoln's mind ";
yet he was not always quick to catch the
President's meaning. Hamilton Fish told
my father about calling upon the President
in Sumner's company when curiosity was
rife over the destination of General Burnside's expedition against Roanoke Island.
Mr. Sumner began asking questions.

" Well," said the President, " I am not
a military man, and of course I cannot tell
about these matters — and indeed, if I did
know, the interests of the public service
require that I should not divulge them.
But," he added, rising and sweeping his
long hand over a map of the North Carolina coast which hung in a corner, " now
see here. Here are a large number of in-
lets, and I should think a fleet might perhaps get in there somewhere. And if they

were to get in there, don't you think our
boys would be likely to cut up some flip-
flaps? I think they would."

Mr. Fish turned the conversation. As
they left the White House Sumner expressed impatience at the President's reti-
cence. " Why," said his companion.
" He told you where Burnside was going!
He wanted to satisfy your curiosity, but of
course he could not make an official declaration. I think you ought to be well
pleased that he was so frank."

" Well, Governor, who has been abusing
me in the Senate to-day? " Lincoln asked
Senator Morrill as the latter came into his
office. The Senator protested.

" Mr. President, I hope none of us abuse
you knowingly and wilfully."

" Oh, well," he said, " I don't mean that.
Personally you are all very kind — but I
know we do not all agree as to what this
administration should do and how it ought
to be done. . . . I do not know but that

God has created some one man great enough to comprehend the whole of this stupendous crisis from beginning to end, and endowed him with sufficient wisdom to manage and direct it. I confess I do not fully understand and foresee it all. But I am placed here where I am obliged to the best of my poor ability to deal with it. And that being the case, I can only go just as fast as I can see how to go."

"That," continued Mr. Morrill, "was the way he saw this thing — as a stupendous movement, which he watched and upon which he acted as he might best do when in his judgment the opportune moment came. . . . He saw that in his dealings with it he must be backed by immense forces; and to this end it was his policy to hold the nation true to the general aim. . . . He moderated, guided, controlled, or pushed ahead as he saw his opportunity. He was the great balance-wheel which held the ship true to her course."

It required all his wisdom, all his firmness, all his tact. He must maintain principles, and not make enemies. A high official came to him in a towering rage, but
went away perfectly satisfied. " I suppose you had to make large concessions? "
the President was asked. " Oh, no," was
the answer. " I did not concede anything.
You have heard how the Illinois farmer
disposed of the log that was too wet to
burn, too big to haul away, and too knotty
to split? He plowed around it. Well,
that is the way I got rid of Governor
Blank. I plowed around him. But it
took three mortal hours; and I was afraid
every minute that he would find me out! "

Lincoln's loyalty and fairness made him
keep unsuccessful generals in command
long after the patience of impatient people
was exhausted. " I think Grant has
hardly a friend left, except myself," he remarked, before the fall of Vicksburg justified the waiting. After Vicksburg fell the

President sent Grant a letter which showed that he too had had his moments of questioning — and also how heartily and gracefully he could say, " You were right and I was wrong."

" My dear General: I do not remember that you and I ever met personally. I write this now as a grateful acknowledgment for the almost inestimable service you have done the country. I wish to say a word further "; then, summing up the various plans that the general had tried in the course of his siege, including the last one which ended in victory, he continued, " When you got below and took Port Gibson, Grand Gulf, and vicinity, I thought you should go down the river and join General Banks, and when you turned northward, east of the Big Black, I feared it was a mistake. I now wish to make the personal acknowledgment that you were right and I was wrong."

The President knew that a change in

commanders always involved more than the mere risk of " swapping horses while crossing a stream." There was the troublesome question of finding a better horse. Senator Wade, who was not the most patient of men, urged him to supplant McClellan.

" Well," said the President, " put yourself in my place for a moment. If I relieve McClellan whom shall I put in command? Who, of all the men, is to supersede him? "

" Why," said Wade, " anybody."

" Wade," replied Mr. Lincoln, with weary resignation, " *anybody* will do for you, but not for me. I must have *somebody*."

He realized that more than mere fighting qualities had to be borne in mind. The multifarious details of keeping an army in good physical and moral condition — from the prompt delivery of rations to good regimental music — and the fact that the lack of one single small item, like horse-shoe nails, might cripple a whole corps and lose a battle, was summed up in his quaint way, when, discussing the qualities of various generals in the field, he said,

"Now there is Joe Hooker. He can fight. I think that is pretty well established — but whether he can 'keep tavern' for a large army is not so sure."

The heart-sickening list of military reputations that began in promise and ended in defeat, dragged on, saddening and wearying him. His inflexible sense of justice left him not even the satisfaction of wrath, for he knew that none of these men failed willingly.

XIII

SECRETARY WELLES kept an interesting and voluminous diary. In it he wrote:

It is an infirmity of the President that he permits the little newsmongers to come around him and be intimate; and in this he is encouraged by Seward, who does the same, and even courts the corrupt and the vicious, which the President does not. He has great inquisitiveness. Likes to hear all the political gossip as much as Seward. But the President is honest, sincere, and confiding. . . .

Fully three-quarters of Lincoln's time was indeed given up to seeing people, and the " little newsmongers " played a not unimportant part in his success. He had no time for reading newspapers. He soon gave up all attempts to do so; yet it was imperative that he should know the drift of thought and feeling all over the country. His private secretaries, bringing him their daily digest of news, marveled to find him already so well informed. The secret lay in these interminable interviews. With prominent men from all sections coming to receive or impart information, and the " plain people," as he liked to call them, coming to him on all sorts of errands, there was hardly a subject of public interest not touched upon and discussed. His visitors supplied all he could have acquired by reading, and in addition the element of interest or prejudice which each unconsciously put into his narrative. The President used to call these interviews his public opinion baths; and he was much better equipped for the task of governing, because he understood, in part at least, the foibles and prejudices of the different localities. He had not left his skill in practical politics behind him in Illinois, and he knew that upon the coöperation of all these people he must finally rely.

His friends begged him to save himself the fatigue of seeing the throngs who came on insignificant errands. They reminded him that nine out of ten had some favor to ask, and that nine-tenths of these he could not grant.

" They do not want much," he answered, " and they get very little. Each one considers his business of great importance, and I must gratify them. I know how I would feel in their place." At noon, on days when the cabinet was not in session, the doors were thrown open, and the public might enter.

There was of course some danger in this. Insane people and criminals might, indeed sometimes did, enter with the rest. But the military guard, the ushers, and Lincoln's secretaries were all on the alert to detect them, and acquired great skill in handling undesirable visitors.

"Lunatics and visionaries are here so frequently that they cease to be strange phenomena," my father wrote. "I find the best way is to discuss and decide their projects as deliberately as any other matter of business."

The President, having read deeply in the book of human nature, was himself skilled in detecting hidden signs of falsehood and deceit. "They are a swindle," the youthful John Hay declared, as he announced a delegation from the far South. "Let them in, they will not swindle me," quoth the President.

Men of all sorts with projects of all kinds, legitimate or otherwise, came to ask for official sanction. These were apt to lag behind, hoping for a word alone with the President. "Well, my friend, what can I do for you?" he would ask in disconcertingly prompt and public fashion. But he arrogated to himself no right of criticism or censure because he was President, treating all as though the burden of proving dishonesty rested upon the Government.

Particularly welcome were the occasional visits of stalwart mountaineers from East Tennessee, whom the President greeted like younger brothers. " He is one of them, really," wrote John Hay; " I never saw him more at his ease than he is with these first-rate patriots of the border."

Sometimes a group of Indians from the far West filled the room with gaudy color, and Lincoln would air his two or three Indian words, to their stolid amusement. Oftener the apartment was somber with the mourning garments of women come to plead for husbands or fathers in trouble, or to ask permission to pass south through the military lines.

More of the President's visitors were sad than happy. Some of them came on errands that were ridiculous as well as trivial. Once a voluble landlady deluged him with insistence that he hold up the pay of her treasury-clerk lodger until his account was settled.

Though so busy he apparently had leisure for all, bending a care-lined benignant face to listen, grave, courteous, sympathetic; breaking at times into his sudden infectious laugh, referring one to this bureau and another to that official, to whom they should have carried their requests in the first place; or scribbling a few words on a card which opened vistas of quite breathless happiness.

It pained him to say " No," and it was his impulse to keep the conversation on a semi-humorous footing where the " No," if it must be said, would hurt as little as possible. To this end he drew on his fund of anecdotes, until almost every account of an interview at the White House tells of the President's smile, and his sympathy, and how he told a funny story.

Sometimes he essayed the dangerous experiment of answering a fool according to his folly. A gentleman came to him in behalf of a private soldier who had knocked down his captain. "I tell you what I will do. You go up to the Capitol, and get Congress to pass a law making it legal for a private to knock down his captain, and I 'll pardon your man with pleasure," he said with such waggish earnestness, and such evident desire to please, that both burst out laughing, and the matter was dropped.

He told his cabinet that he found certain questions very embarrassing. He reminded himself of a man in Illinois who was so annoyed by a pressing creditor that he feigned insanity whenever the creditor broached the subject. "I," said the President, "on more than one occasion in this

263

room, have been compelled to appear very mad."

The few people who had no requests to make, usually came to give advice. Ministers seemed to feel themselves as privileged as Senators in this regard. Mr. Carpenter tells of a clergyman who asked for an interview. The President assumed an air of patient waiting. There was a moment's silence. " I am now ready to hear what you have to say," he prompted, as the silence continued. The visitor hastily disclaimed having anything particular to say. He had only come to pay his respects. " My dear sir! " the other cried, his face lighting up, " I am delighted to see you. I thought you had come to preach to me! "

Singly or in delegations they came for that purpose — to show him his duty in regard to emancipation, or some other matter about which he was not yet ready to declare his policy. While courteous, he absolutely refused to be hurried into a declaration. "He will not be bullied, even by his friends," one of his secretaries wrote.

Others, singly, or in delegations, came to pray with him. Respecting their motive, and himself deeply religious, he received them with unfailing courtesy. A Methodist exhortation, or a Quaker prayer meeting, might seem inconvenient, even time consuming, in the midst of his busy morning, but this "Christian without a creed" not only reverenced the power to whom the petition was addressed; he was grateful for the human bond it helped to strengthen. Sometimes, however, he was moved to ask questions hard to meet. To one person who claimed to bring him a direct command from the Almighty, he replied:

"I hope it will not be irreverent for me to say that if it is probable that God would reveal his will to others on a point so connected with my duty, it might be supposed He would reveal it directly to me."

He had a most disconcerting way of pricking bubbles with the point of his logic. A committee of rich New Yorkers hurried to Washington when the Confederate ironclad *Merrimac* was striking terror into hearts along the Atlantic coast, and demanded a gun-boat for the protection of New York harbor. " Gentlemen," he answered, " the credit of the Government is at a very low ebb. It is impossible under present conditions to do what you ask. But it seems to me, that if I were half as rich as you are reputed to be, and half as badly scared as you appear to be, I would build a gun-boat and present it to the Government."

When, at long intervals, his patience gave way, and he blazed forth in righteous wrath, men quailed before him. Editor Medill of the Chicago *Tribune* told of a time in 1864 when a call for extra troops drove Chicago to the verge of revolt. Her quota was 6000 men. She sent a delegation to ask for a new enrollment, which Stanton refused. Lincoln consented to go with the delegation to Stanton's office and hear both sides. " I shall never forget," said Mr. Medill, " how after sitting in silence for some time, he suddenly lifted his head and turned on us a black and frowning face.

" ' Gentlemen,' he said, in a voice full of bitterness, ' after Boston, Chicago has been the chief instrument in bringing this war on the country. The Northwest has opposed the South as the Northeast has opposed the South. It is you who are largely responsible for making blood flow as it has. You called for war until we had it. You called for emancipation, and I have given it to you. Whatever you have asked for you have had. Now you come here begging to be let off from the call for men which I have made to carry on

the war you have demanded. You ought
to be ashamed of yourselves. I have a
right to expect better things of you. And
you, Medill, you are acting like a coward.
You and your *Tribune* have had more influence than any paper in the Northwest
in making this war. You can influence
great masses, and yet you cry to be spared
at a moment when your cause is suffering.
Go home and send us those men!'

"I could n't say anything. It was the
first time I was ever whipped, and I did n't
have an answer. We all got up and went
out, and when the door closed, one of my
colleagues said, 'Well, gentlemen, the Old
Man is right. We ought to be ashamed of
ourselves. Let us never say anything
about this, but go home and raise the
men.'"

It speaks volumes for Lincoln's absolute justice and for Medill's fairminded-
ness, that even after the lapse of years, the
editor could bring himself to tell how

Lincoln called him " coward," and admit
that he was right.

Usually the President sat out impor-
tunity in an attitude of patient waiting.
One summer afternoon General Fry found
him listening to a common soldier. He
looked worn and tired. " Well, my man,
that may all be so, but you must go to
your officers about it," he said when the
petitioner stopped for breath. Again the
tale recommenced, and the President gazed
wearily through his office window at the
broad river in the distance. Finally he
turned to him out of patience.

" Go away," he said. " Now *go away*.
I cannot meddle in your case. I could as
easily bail out the Potomac with a tea-
spoon as attend to all the details of the
army."

It was not often that he showed even
so much feeling. Ordinarily he trusted
to the soft answer which turns away wrath,
or to the humorous answer which disarms

resentment. The wittiest of all of these he made in answering a man who wanted a pass to Richmond.

"I would gladly give you the pass if it would do you any good," he said. "But in the last two years I have given passes to Richmond to 250,000 men, and not one of them has managed to get there yet."

But even wit did not make refusal easy to this kind-hearted man. He extracted a grim amusement from his attack of varioloid by saying that at last he "had something he could give to everybody!"

Once in a while he had the pleasant surprise of a visitor with something important and helpful to say. At the time he was considering a proclamation of amnesty, Mr. Robert Dale Owen took it upon himself to prepare a digest of historical precedents. He spent three months upon the task, and then asked permission to read his paper to the President. Mr. Lincoln, knowing nothing of its contents, and secing only a very formidable-looking document, settled into his attitude of patient endurance. But this soon gave way to alert interest. He began asking questions, and interrupting with requests that certain paragraphs be read again. When Mr. Owen finished, and offered him the paper, he accepted it with hearty thanks.

" Mr. Owen, it is due to you that I should say that you have conferred a very essential service both upon me and upon the country by the preparation of this paper. It contains that which it was exceedingly important that I should know, but which, if left to myself, I never should have known, because I have not the time necessary for such an examination of authorities as a review of this kind involves. And I want to say, secondly, that if I had the time, I could not have done the work as well as you have done it."

Nothing showed his patience and kindliness more than his manner with the women

271

who came to the Executive Office — and
many were the militant females he encoun-
tered during his Presidency.

" To-day, Mrs. Major Blank of the regular army calls and urges the appointment
of her husband as a brigadier-general.
She is a saucy woman, and I am afraid
she will keep tormenting me till I may
have to do it," is his autograph confession
of a spirited feminine attack; and of their
inequality of weapons.

The wife of a Western general, more energetic than diplomatic, descended upon
the capital, demanded an interview with
the President, and upbraided him with
meaning to ruin her husband. Lincoln began to talk about the difficulty she must
have experienced in making the journey
from the West alone; more of a journey
then than now. He was so kind that she
had to respond, but she was very persistent, and very much in earnest, and had
no idea of stopping there. Again and

again she returned to the charge; again and again he parried. He was courteous, even sympathetic, but he took no notice of her questions or insinuations, and gave her not a single answer. "I had to exercise all the rude tact I have, to. avoid quarreling with her," he said feelingly when the ordeal was over.

But it was in dealing with women in distress, particularly with women in the humbler walks of life, that his kindness was most marked.

"It is hard to portray the exquisite pathos of Mr. Lincoln's character, as manifested in his acts from time to time," Mr. James Speed once said to my father, in telling him of an incident that had come to his knowledge. It was at the end of one of the daily receptions.

"Is that all?" Mr. Lincoln asked.

"There is one poor woman here yet, Mr. President," Edward, the colored usher, replied. "She has been here for several days and has been crying and taking on, and has n't got a chance to come in yet."

" Let her in," said Mr. Lincoln.

The woman told her story. It was just after the battle of Gettysburg. She had a husband and three sons in the army, and was left alone to fight the hard battle of life. At first her husband had sent her regularly a part of his pay, and she had managed to live. But gradually he had yielded to the temptations of camp life, and no more remittances came. Her boys had become scattered among the various armies, and she was without help. Would not the President discharge one of them that he might come home to her?

While the recital was going on the President stood before the fireplace, his hands crossed behind his back, his head bent in earnest thought. When the woman ended, and waited for his reply, his lips opened and he spoke, not as if he were replying to what she said, but rather as if he were in abstracted and unconscious self-communion.

" I have two, and you have none."

That was all he said. Then he walked across to his writing table, and taking a blank card, wrote upon it an order for the son's discharge. Upon another paper he wrote out in great detail where she should present it, to what department, at what office, and to what official; giving her such directions that she might personally follow the red-tape labyrinth.

A few days later, at a similar close of the general reception for the day, Edward said, " That woman, Mr. President, is here again, and still crying."

" Let her in," said Lincoln. " What can be the matter now? "

Once more he stood in the same spot, before the fireplace, and for the second time heard her story. The President's card had been a magic passport. It had opened forbidden doors, and softened the sternness of official countenances. By its help she had found headquarters, camp, regiment and company. But instead of giving a mother's embrace to a lost son restored, she had arrived only in time to follow him to the grave. The battle of Gettysburg, his wounds, his death in the hospital — the story came in eloquent fragments through her ill-stifled sobs. And now, would the President give her the next one of her boys?

Once more Mr. Lincoln responded with sententious curtness, as if talking to himself,

" I have two, and you have none."

Sharp and rather stern, the compression of his lips marking the struggle between official duty and human sympathy, he walked once again to his little writing table and took up his pen to write for the second time an order which should give the pleading woman one of her remaining boys.

And the woman, as if in obedience to an impulse she could not control, moved after him, and stood by his side as he wrote, and with the familiarity of a mother placed her hand on the President's head and smoothed his wandering and tangled hair. Human grief and sympathy had overleapt all the barriers of convention, and the ruler of a great nation was truly the servant, friend, and protector of this humble woman, clothed for the moment with a paramount claim of loyal sacrifice.

The order was written and signed. The President rose and thrust it into her hand with the choking exclamation, " There! " and hurried from the room, followed, so long as he could hear, by the thanks and blessings of an overjoyed mother's heart.

Lincoln's sympathy for the soldiers was very genuine. They were not only fighting his country's battles — they came from that large mass of sturdy citizenship of which he spoke with pride and affection as "the common people." "With us every soldier is a man of character, and must be treated with more consideration than is customary in Europe," he explained to a French nobleman.

He recognized the potential force in each single regiment. "I happen temporarily to occupy the White House. I am a living witness that any one of your children may look to come here as my father's child has," he told an Ohio regiment; and another time he remarked that any regiment of the army could furnish material and ability to fill all the highest offices in the Government.

His visits to camps and army corps were an ovation, for the "boys" loved him in return, and responded in every way permitted by discipline. It was not only for soldiers in the abstract that he cared. He sampled their rations, chuckled over their repartee, and "sized up" individual members of a company as he passed by; while for those in trouble he agonized in spirit as no ruler of this world had ever done.

Court-martial cases reached a number approaching 30,000 a year during the war; and although, of course, only a small proportion were for capital offenses, the latter were referred by hundreds to President Lincoln; and each case brought to his notice became the subject of his personal solicitude. Secretary Stanton and officers of the army protested against his wholesale clemency. He would ruin the army, they declared; but the military telegraph was kept busy with his messages staying executions and asking details of evidence. Attorney-General Bates told him flatly that he was not fit to be entrusted with the pardoning power. This did not move him in the least. He privately believed Bates to be as " pigeon-hearted " as himself.

Judge-Advocate General Holt labored
with him, pointing out why it was better
rigidly to enforce the law. "Yes, your
reasons are very good," he would reply,
"but I don't think I can do it." He
"did not believe it would make a man any
better to shoot him," and argued that if
the Government kept him alive it could
at least get some work out of him.

He used to tell his story of the Irish
soldier who was asked why he had deserted. "Well, Captain," said he, "it
was not me fault. I've a heart in me
breast as brave as Julius Cæsar; but when
the battle begins, somehow or other these
cowardly legs of mine will run away wid
me!"

"I have no doubt," the President would
add, "that is true of many a man who
honestly means to do his duty, but is over-
come by a physical fear greater than his
will. I am not sure how I would act myself if Minie balls were whistling, and

those great oblong shells were shrieking in my ears."

He used to call cases of cowardice and desertion his "leg cases." In the press of business large numbers of them accumulated on his desk; when he had leisure he would send for Judge Holt and go over them. John Hay, making record in his diary of six hours of a July day spent in this manner, commented on the eagerness with which Mr. Lincoln caught at any fact which would justify saving the life of a condemned soldier. He was only merciless in cases where meanness or cruelty were shown. "Cases of cowardice he was especially averse to punishing with death. He said it would frighten the poor devils too terribly to shoot them." "Let him fight instead of shooting him," he endorsed on the case of a man who had once before deserted, and then reënlisted.

The sentence of another who had safely escaped into Mexico he approved, saying,

"We will condemn him as they sell hogs in Indiana, ' as they run.' "

Schuyler Colfax, happening on such a scene, carried away a memory of Lincoln's exceeding reluctance to approve the death penalty. One case he laid aside, saying he would wait a few days until he could read the evidence. Another he put by " until I can settle in my mind whether this soldier can better serve the country dead or living." To still a third he said that the general commanding would be in Washington soon, and he would talk it over with him. At last Judge Holt presented a very flagrant case, with the remark that this might meet the President's requirement of serving the country better dead than living; but Lincoln answered that, anyway, he guessed he 'd put it among his " leg cases."

Some of the reasons he gave for granting pardons were whimsical enough, but there was a sound principle underlying his action. He tried to probe for motives; and if he learned that a man's general record was good, he accepted that as presumptive evidence that he meant to do right, wherever his "cowardly legs" might have carried him.

"This life is too precious to be lost," he said in the case of a boy who fell asleep on guard because in addition to his own duty, he had volunteered to take the place of a sick comrade.

"Did you say this boy was once badly wounded? Then, since the Scriptures say that in the shedding of blood is remission of sins, I guess we 'll have to let him off," was his decree in another case. "If a man had more than one life I think a little hanging would not hurt this one," he said again. "But after he is once dead we cannot bring him to life, no matter how sorry we may be; so the boy shall be pardoned," and resting a moment from his labors, he threw up his spectacles, and told

283

his story of a darky in one of the bravest regiments at Fort Donelson.

"Were you in the fight?" some one asked him.

"Had a little taste ob it, sah."

"Stood your ground, did you?"

"No, sah — I runs."

"Ran at the first fire, did you?"

"Yes, sah, an' I would 'a run sooner if I knowed it was a-comin'."

"That was not very creditable to your courage."

"Dat is n't my line, sah. Cookin' is my perfession."

"But have you no regard for your reputation?"

"Reputation 's nuffin to me by de side ob life."

"Do you consider your life worth more than other peoples'?"

"Worth mo' to me, sah."

"Do you think your company would have missed you if you had been killed?"

284

" Maybe not, sah. A dead white man ain' much to dese sojers, let alone a dead nigger. But I 'd 'a' missed myself, an' dat 's de point wif me."

Many of Lincoln's daily visitors came on these sad errands. Congressmen appealed to him to pardon their constituents. " Why don't you men up there in Congress repeal the law, instead of coming and asking me to override it and make it practically a dead letter? " he asked. But they did not see fit to do so, and he plodded wearily through endless masses of testimony.

It was in this labor that he spent the morning after his reëlection. He became more and more convinced of the sickening uselessness of " this butchering business." " There are already too many weeping widows in the United States," he said. " For God's sake do not ask me to add to the number! " and he almost invariably suspended execution " until further or-

ders," which, needless to say, were never
given.

"If a man comes to him with a touching
story, his judgment is almost certain to
be affected by it. Should the applicant
be a woman — a wife, mother, or sister —
in nine cases out of ten, her tears, if nothing else, are sure to prevail," Attorney-
General Bates declared.

The most whimsical reason sufficed.

"My poor girl," he said to a young
woman in a neat but scanty dress, "you
have come with no governor or senator or
member of Congress to plead your cause.
You seem truthful, and *you don't wear
hoops*, and I'll be whipped but I'll pardon
your brother!"

Some of these cases came very close to
him personally, as he read the names of
men or sons of men he had known; but
even when no personal acquaintance intensified his interest, the care he bestowed
upon them was enormous. Not only one

telegram, but several would be sent about a single case. Some of them, long and full of detail, betrayed the strain to which his sympathy had been subjected. One, to General Mead, was as follows:

An intelligent woman in deep distress called this morning, saying her husband, a lieutenant in the Army of the Potomac, was to be shot next Monday for desertion; and putting a letter in my hand, upon which I relied for particulars, she left me without mentioning a name or other particular by which to identify the case. On opening the letter I found it equally vague, having nothing to identify her by except her signature, which seems to be " Mrs. Anna S. King." I could not again find her. If you have a case which you shall think is probably the one intended, please apply my despatch of this morning to it.

His " despatch of this morning " was his usual order to postpone execution till further orders.

ABRAHAM LINCOLN

Thaddeus Stevens once went with a constituent of his, an elderly woman, to the President on an errand of mercy. Mr. Lincoln granted her request, and her gratitude was literally too deep for words. Not a syllable did she utter until they were well on their way out of the White House, when she stood still and broke forth vehemently:

"I knew it was a Copperhead lie!"

"What do you mean, madam?" he asked.

"They told me that he was an ugly-looking man! He is not. He is the handsomest man I ever saw in my life!"

XIV

" I AM here by the blunders of the Democrats," Lincoln told Hugh McCulloch. " If, instead of resolving that the war was a failure, they had resolved that I was a failure, and denounced me for not more vigorously prosecuting it, I should not have been reëlected."

No act or episode of his life was more characteristic than his attitude toward a second term. In talking with strangers he discouraged any mention of it, but to friends he frankly admitted his readiness to continue the work he had entered upon. " A second term would be a great honor, and a great labor, which together, perhaps, I would not decline if tendered."

His two secretaries were, of course, keenly interested; and the way he pursued his undeviating course, not indifferent to, but regardless of, his political fate, would have won their undying admiration, had it not been his long before.

" This town is now as dismal as a defaced tombstone," John Hay wrote my father late in the summer of 1863. " The Tycoon is in fine whack. I have rarely seen him so serene and so busy. He is managing this war, the draft, foreign relations, and planning a reconstruction of the Union, all in one. I never knew with what tyrannous authority he rules the cabinet until now. The most important things he decides, and there is no cavil. I am growing more and more firmly convinced that the good of the country absolutely demands that he should be kept where he is till this thing blows over.

There is no man in the country so wise, so gentle and so firm. I believe the hand of God placed him where he is."

"Some well-meaning newspapers advise the President to keep his fingers out of the military pie, and all that sort of thing," he wrote again; "the truth is, if he did, the pie would be a sorry mess. The old man sits here and wields like a backwoods Jupiter the bolts of war and the machinery of Government, with a hand equally steady and equally firm. . . . I do not know whether the nation is worthy of him for another term. I know the people want him. There is no mistaking that fact. But politicians are strong yet and he is not 'their kind of a cat.' I hope God won't see fit to scourge us for our sins by any one of the two or three most prominent candidates on the ground. . . ."

Republicans generally felt as did these two young men, but the President had active critics and opponents within his own party. " Corruption, intrigue and malice are doing their worst, but I do not think it is in the cards to beat the Tycoon," my father wrote in his turn. Curiously enough, the most determined opposition within Republican ranks came from anti-slavery men, who could not forgive the Emancipator for the deliberation with which he took the steps toward freedom. There were also those who blamed him for the slow progress of the war.

It was hard, however, for these elements of discontent to find a rallying point, since no prominent Republican in Congress or in the military service cared to enter the ungrateful contest. In the cabinet only one man was short-sighted enough to imagine he could make headway against Lincoln's wide popularity. This was Chase, who had been the first to assure Lincoln of his support in 1860. Pure minded and absolutely devoted to the Union though he was, he seemed incapable of judging men or motives — even his own — correctly. He really thought himself free from political ambition, and truly Lincoln's friend, yet for months he was busy writing letters in the interests of his own candidacy.

Lincoln knew of this, but went on appointing Mr. Chase's partizans to office. John Hay, wrathfully indignant, ventured to free his mind to his chief, telling him he was making himself *particeps criminis* by these appointments. "He seemed much amused at Chase's mad hunt after the Presidency," the young man wrote. "He says it may win. He hopes the country will never do worse."

The movement in Chase's favor reached its culmination in a secret circular signed by a committee of which Senator Pomeroy of Kansas was chairman, which criticized Lincoln's "tendency toward compromises and temporary expedients" and lauded Chase as the man to rescue the country

from present and future ills. Copies of
this soon reached the White House. Lincoln refused to look at them. Shortly
afterward it got into print. Secretary
Chase wrote to the President offering to
resign, but assuring him that he had no
knowledge of the document before seeing
it in the newspapers.

Mr. Robert Lincoln remembers that he
was at home at the time, and that after
dinner his father strolled into his room,
showed him Mr. Chase's letter, asked for
writing materials, and sitting down wrote
a note in answer, to the effect that he knew
just as little about such things as his
friends allowed him to know, that neither
of them could be held responsible for acts
committed without their instigation or approval, and adding, "Whether you shall
remain at the head of the Treasury Department is a question which I will not
allow myself to consider from any stand-
point other than my judgment of the pub-

lic service, and, in that view, I do not perceive occasion for a change."

When he showed this to his son, the latter asked in surprise if he had not seen the circular. Mr. Lincoln stopped him almost sternly, saying that a good many people had tried to tell him something it did not suit him to hear, and that his answer to the Secretary of the Treasury was literally true. " Thereupon," Mr. Robert Lincoln added, " at his request I called a messenger, and the note to Mr. Chase was sent."

Mr. Chase's candidacy, however, had no foundation except in the imagination of a few personal followers, and perished for lack of nourishment. An attempt, made without Grant's knowledge, to stampede the country for that general, failed for the same reason. Lincoln regarded that also with the utmost serenity. " If he takes Richmond, let him have it," he said.

But the talk annoyed him. " I wish they

would stop thrusting that subject of the Presidency into my face," he remarked. " I don't want to hear anything about it."

It was neither Chase nor Grant, but Fremont who was finally nominated by Republican malcontents in a much-heralded but poorly attended convention at Cleveland. Lincoln, on hearing that most of the expected leaders stayed away, and that at no time was the attendance greater than four hundred, picked up the Bible which lay habitually on his desk, and after turning over the leaves a moment read:

" And every one that was in debt, and every one that was discontented, gathered themselves unto him; and he became a captain over them, and there were with him about four hundred men."

The great current had set toward Lincoln, and when the Republican National Convention came together in Baltimore on the 7th of June, 1864, it had nothing to do but to record the popular will. The choice of a Vice-president presented more difficulty, for there was an impression abroad that it would be wise to select a war Democrat. Lincoln was besieged to make his wishes known, but refused, even to his closest friends, being convinced that it was a question in which he had absolutely no right to interfere. The final choice was made so quickly that the President, walking over to the War Department, in quest of news, heard of Andrew Johnson's nomination before the messenger despatched a few minutes earlier, with a telegram announcing his own renomination, had succeeded in finding him.

Next day, for the second time in his life, this pioneer ruler faced a committee sent to tell him that he had been nominated for the highest office within the people's gift. This time he received them in the great East Room instead of in his modest Springfield parlor. He, as well as his surroundings, was altered. Experience had ripened him, responsibility had aged him. His benignity of expression was greater, his physical vigor less. There was in his bearing all the old courage, and a greater consciousness of power.

The summer proved to be full of fighting and frightful losses in the armies, and of consequent panics among politicians. It became necessary to resort to a draft, and this in itself indicated such waning enthusiasm that leading Republicans begged the President to withdraw the call, or at least to suspend it until after the election. " What is the Presidency worth to me, if I have no country? " was his answer.

He brought serious criticism upon himself by refusing to sign a bill passed by Congress which prescribed a form for re-establishing State governments based on the assumption that they had been out of the Union. Lincoln's contention from the first had been that the Union was perpetual, and that they had never passed, and could not pass by revolution, out of Federal control. It was, he admitted, " a question of metaphysics," but it involved the principle on which all his action had been based, and which he could not ignore, even though it might have serious consequences for himself.

The Peace men, meanwhile, were clamoring for an end of the war. Horace Greeley insisted with such vehemence that Confederate commissioners already were in Canada, empowered and ready to treat with the Federal authorities, that Lincoln, to convince him and others like-minded that the administration was as anxious as they could be to bring the war to a close, empowered Greeley himself to go to Canada, and if he found the alleged commissioners properly authorized, to bring them to Washington. The mission ended as Lincoln supposed it would, in proving the utter falsity of Greeley's assertions, and in making that earnest gentleman a bit ridiculous.

"I sent Brother Greeley a commission. I guess I am about even with him," he said with a twinkle in his eye.

But all these causes combined to increase the popular unrest, and to breed dissatisfaction with the administration. McClellan seemed the foreordained Democratic candidate, but the party managers, realizing the advantage of making their opponents fight an unseen foe, and at the same time of keeping themselves in a position to drop McClellan and adopt some one else if chance and the fortunes of war dictated, postponed their national convention until September; and having no candidate of their own, were free to devote all their time and energy to attacks upon the administration.

In the campaign of 1860 Lincoln had possessed no shadow of authority. Now that he commanded all the resources of the

Government, he was implored to make promises, to assist his friends and oppose his enemies.

"I recognize no such thing as political friendship personal to myself," he answered, and as far as promises were concerned, he kept himself as free as he had done four years before when he announced that he would go to Washington "an unpledged man."

One who was present related to my father the details of a stormy interview which took place between the President, Simon Cameron and Thaddeus Stevens. They had come to talk over the political situation in Pennsylvania. Mr. Stevens said: "Mr. President, our convention at Baltimore has nominated you again, and not only that, we are going to elect you. But the certainty of that will depend very much on the vote we can give you in Pennsylvania in October; and in order that we may be able in our State to go to work with a good will I want you to make us one promise; namely, that you will reorganize your cabinet and leave Montgomery Blair out of it."

Mr. Stevens went on to elaborate his reasons, and a running fire of criticism and comment was entered into between the three gentlemen, gradually rising in warmth; the whole interview lasting some two or three hours. As the discussion proceeded, Mr. Lincoln rose from his chair and walked up and down the room.

The issue being made up, he gave his answer, towering to his full height, and delivering his words with emphatic gestures and intense earnestness.

" Mr. Stevens, I am very sorry to be compelled to deny your request to make such a promise. If I were even myself inclined to make it, I have no right to do so. What right have I to promise you to remove Mr. Blair, and not make a similar promise to any other gentleman of influence to remove any other member of my cabinet whom he does not happen to like? The Republican party wisely or unwisely has made me their nominee for President, without asking any such pledge at my hands. Is it proper that you should demand it, representing only a portion of that great party? Has it come to this, that the voters of this country are asked to elect a man to be President — to be Executive — to administer the Government, and yet that this man is to have no will or discretion of his own? Am I to be the mere puppet of power? To have my constitutional advisers selected beforehand, to be told I must do this, or leave that undone? It would be degrading to my manhood to consent to any such bargain — I was about to say it is equally degrading to your manhood to ask it.

" I confess that I desire to be reëlected. God knows I do not want the labor and responsibility of the office for another four years. But I have the common pride of humanity to wish my past four years' administration endorsed; and besides I honestly believe that I can better serve the nation in its need and peril than any new man could possibly do. I want to finish this job of putting down the rebellion, and restoring peace and prosperity to the country. But I would have the courage to refuse the office rather than to accept on such disgraceful terms as really not to be President after I am elected."

The political horizon grew darker and darker. Military victory, which would have rejoiced all hearts and turned the current toward Republican success, was denied. Lincoln grew haggard and careworn. To a friend who urged him to go away for a fortnight's rest, he replied, " I cannot fly from my thoughts. My solicitude for this great country follows me wherever I go. I do not think it is personal vanity or ambition, though I am not free from these infirmities, but I cannot but feel that the weal or woe of this great nation will be decided in November. There is no program offered by any wing of the Democratic party but that must result in the permanent destruction of the Union."

Toward the end of August he became convinced that the election was likely to go against him. Having come to this conclusion, he laid down for himself in writing the course he ought to pursue. On the 23d he wrote:

"This morning, as for some days past, it seems exceedingly probable that this administration will not be reëlected. Then it will be my duty to so coöperate with the President-elect as to save the Union between the election and the inauguration, as he will have secured his election on such ground that he cannot possibly save it afterward."

He folded and pasted the sheet of paper

in such a way that its contents were hidden, and as the members of the cabinet came in, handed it to each in turn, asking them to write their names across the back. Then he put the paper away, giving no hint of its nature.

Two days later my father wrote to John Hay, who was in Illinois:

DEAR MAJOR: Hell is to pay. The New York politicians have got a stampede on that is about to swamp everything. Raymond and the National Committee are here to-day. R. thinks a commission to Richmond is about the only salt to save us; while the Tycoon sees and says it would be utter ruination. The matter is now undergoing consultation. Weak-kneed d—d fools . . . are in the movement for a new candidate to supplant the Tycoon. Everything is darkness and doubt and discouragement. Our men see giants in the airy and unsubstantial shadows of the opposition, and are about to surrender without a fight.

AUGUST TWENTY-THIRD

I think that to-day and here is the turning-point in our crisis. If the President can infect R. and his committee with some of his own patience and pluck, we are saved. If our friends will only rub their eyes and shake themselves, and become convinced that they themselves are not dead, we shall win the fight overwhelmingly.

Henry J. Raymond was Chairman of the Executive Committee of the Republican party. Mr. Lincoln answered his proposal to send a commission to Richmond by the same kindergarten method he had used in answering Greeley. He asked Mr. Raymond to draw up an experimental draft of resolutions which he proposed that Mr. Raymond should himself carry to Richmond. On seeing them in black and white the mission took on a different aspect, and Raymond readily agreed that such a course would be worse than losing the election — it would be surrendering it in advance.

" Nevertheless," wrote the President's secretary, " the visit of himself and committee did great good. They found the President and cabinet much better informed than themselves, and went home encouraged and cheered."

That proved indeed to be the turning-point of the campaign. A few days later the Democrats nominated McClellan upon a platform declaring the war to be a failure. That in itself was fatal to their cause, since McClellan's one chance of success lay in his war record. " The Lord preserve this country from the kind of peace they would give us! It will be a dark day for this nation if they elect the Chicago ticket!" wrote an inmate of the White House.

McClellan himself was apparently somewhat aghast. He did not reply to the letter from the Convention for some days. Lincoln was asked what he thought could be the cause of the delay. " Oh," he said, " he 's intrenching."

Military and naval victories began to succeed the discouragements of the preceding months; the country awoke to the true meaning of the Democratic platform; and in a brilliant rush of enthusiasm and hope the political campaign went on to its triumphant end with Republican majorities so incredibly large that one patriot remarked in the utmost reverence, that " The Almighty himself must have stuffed the ballot-boxes."

The night of election day was rainy and dark. The President splashed through puddles to the War Department to get the returns, and sent the interesting despatches back to Mrs. Lincoln at the White House, saying, " She is more anxious than I am."

He was not alone as he had been four years before when the telegraph instruments ticked news of his victory, and the appalling sense of his responsibility had blotted out the noise of cheering in the streets. This election was a vindication of the way he had borne his trust; the verdict of the people that they held him worthy to complete his task. Officials and friends came and went as he read the returns. He was "most genial and agreeable all the evening," and when a midnight supper appeared from some beneficent and mysterious source, he took the part of host, and "went awkwardly and hospitably to work," serving the fried oysters. He told stories, and was gay and happy, yet there was no lack of feeling, even of deep solemnity, in the closing words of the little speech he made to the serenaders he found waiting for him when he left the War Department in the early morning hours to return to the White House:

"I am thankful to God for this approval of the people; but while deeply grateful for this mark of their confidence in me, if I know my heart, my gratitude is free from any taint of personal triumph. . . . It is no pleasure to me to triumph over any one; but I give thanks to the Almighty for this evidence of the people's resolution to stand by free government and the rights of humanity."

At the next cabinet meeting the President took a paper from his desk. It had a series of autographs across the back. " Gentlemen," he said, " do you remember last summer I asked you to sign your names to the back of a paper of which I did not show you the inside? This is it. Now, Mr. Hay, see if you can get this open without tearing it." It required some little cutting to get it open. Then he read the memorandum of August 23d with its signature, A. Lincoln, and the names on the outside, William H. Seward, W. P. Fessenden, Edwin M. Stanton, Gideon Welles, Edw. Bates, M. Blair, and J. P. Usher.

"You will remember," he said, "that this was written at a time six days before the Chicago nominating convention, when as yet we had no adversary, and seemed to have no friends. I then solemnly resolved on the course of action indicated above. I resolved in case of the election of General McClellan, being certain that he would be the candidate, that I would see him and talk matters over with him. I would say, 'General, the election has demonstrated that you are stronger and have more influence with the American people than I. Now let us together, you with your influence, and I with all the executive power of the Government, try to save the country. You raise as many troops as you possibly can for this final trial, and I will devote all my energies to assisting and finishing the war.'"

One of his hearers said, "And the general would answer you, 'Yes, Yes'; and the next day when you saw him again, and

Executive Mansion
Washington, Aug. 23, 1864.

This morning, as for some days past, it seems exceedingly probable that this Administration will not be re-elected. Then it will be my duty to so co-operate with the President elect, as to save the Union between the election and the inauguration; as he will have secured his election on such ground that he can not possibly save it afterwards.

A. Lincoln

William H Seward
W P Fessenden
Edwin M Stanton
William Dennison
Edwd Bates
M Blair
J P Usher

August 23 1864.

Memorandum across the Back of which Lincoln asked His Cabinet to write Their Names, but Whose Contents he did not show Them until after His Re-election

pressed those views upon him, he would say, ' Yes, Yes,' and so on forever, and would have done nothing at all."

" At least," said the President, " I should have done my duty and have stood clear before my own conscience."

Just when one feels that one has Lincoln's traits classified — that he was a very kind man with a keenly logical mind and a buoyant disposition — a man with ideals but no illusions, who saw things without glamor, and patiently looked ahead to plan and combine them to his will, one comes upon some such contradiction as this.

Why did he write such a paper as this memorandum of August 23, 1864? And, having written it, why did he paste it together and get his cabinet to write their names across the back, ignorant of its contents?

What hidden comfort did he expect to derive from this — or what possible use could he have made of it if the nightmare of his defeat had come true? He was sure of his own steadfastness, sure of the loyalty of his cabinet. Why resort to this unpractical but most characteristic act?

Was it that while he had the courage to stand alone — to bear his burden silently without adding to the gloom and discouragement of even his closest advisers — he wrote this and got them to set their names upon it as a sort of silent witness of his secret pledge — that though he meant to go down in defeat, if he must, " like the Cumberland, with colors flying," he craved for himself the sympathy he gave in such unstinted measure to others?

XV

ON the day of Lincoln's second election the White House was still and deserted. "Everybody in Washington, and not at home voting, seems ashamed of it, and stays away from the President," John Hay wrote. Sitting in this unwonted leisure, Lincoln's deep-set eyes looked back over the thirty-two years of his political life. After a time he said: "It is a little singular that I, who am not a vindictive man, should have always been before the people for election in canvasses marked for their bitterness. Always but once. When I came to Congress it was a quiet time. . . . "

ABRAHAM LINCOLN

At the end of the vista he saw a lank, unknown youth of twenty-three, carefully signing his name to his first public paper, an " Address to the Voters of Sangamon County," which was a territory larger than the State of Rhode Island, and as far removed from the center of political life as the equator is from the pole. The friend to whom he spoke saw a gaunt, care-worn figure, aging before his time, whose sad benignant face was known to the world's end; and whose name, written with equal care at the foot of a state paper not long before, had set four million people free. These thirty-two years had covered a period of material development as great as that of any century preceding it, and keeping pace with this, the political activities in which he had taken part had ranged from the purely local needs of a frontier community to the moral problems which have shaken empires and made martyrs since the world began.

HIS FORGIVING SPIRIT

That he passed through these without engendering spite in himself or enmity in his opponents shows that he was indeed "not a vindictive man." There was a Quaker.strain in his blood. His father had been called lazy. If Lincoln inherited any of this trait it was transmuted both by his Quaker blood and by the kindness in his heart into a laziness about making quarrels. That night of his second election the group gathered in the War Department, jubilant over the returns, yet

ngs about cer-
en hostile to the
re of that feel-
than I have,"
'Perhaps I have
thought it paid.
o spend half his
nan ceases to at-
r the past against

reason why, according to the daily press, "intimate friends" of the great President have been dying with alarming frequency for forty years. He was so kindly that people felt "intimate" with him on very slight acquaintance.

That friends were a better political and worldly asset than enemies, a logic less keen than his could easily prove; yet it is safe to say that it was his heart rather than his head which made him strive, all his life long, to turn enemies into friends.

He did not like strife. In his merchant days he preserved the decencies of his shop by knocking down a ruffian who insisted on swearing in the presence of women, and he emphasized the lesson by rubbing a plentiful supply of dog-fennel into his cheeks, but when the man howled for mercy Lincoln brought water to bathe his smarting face.

With the exception of his one duel he was never engaged in a political quarrel.

HIS FORGIVING SPIRIT

In 1840 a man named Anderson with whom he was contesting a seat in the legislature sent him a note bristling with belligerent possibilities. Lincoln's answer ended the matter, though it was more of an apology to himself than to his correspondent.

In the difficulty between us of which you speak you say you think I was the aggressor. I do not think I was. You say my " words imported insult." I meant them as a fair set-off to your own statements and not otherwise; and in that light alone I now wish you to understand them. You ask for my " present feelings on the subject." I entertain no un-kind feelings to you, and none of any sort upon the subject, except a sincere regret that I permitted myself to get into such an altercation.

In maturer life his attitude was ever the same. While he was President it became his official duty to reprimand a young officer court-martialed for quarreling. No gentler rebuke was ever administered.

ABRAHAM LINCOLN

The advice of a father to his son, " Beware of entrance to a quarrel, but being in, bear it that the opposed may beware of thee," is good, but not the best. Quarrel not at all. No man, resolved to make the most of himself, can spare the time for personal contention. Still less can he afford to take all the consequences, including the vitiating of his temper, and the loss of self-control. Yield larger things to which you can show no more than equal right; and yield lesser ones though clearly your own. Better give your path to a dog than be bitten by him in contesting for the right. Even killing the dog would not cure the bite.

The sweet reasonableness of turning the other cheek is not often urged.

His sense of humor, and his failure to take himself too seriously, gave him all the more time and strength for things which really mattered, but led his friends at times into questionable liberties of speech. General John M. Palmer once said to him,

" Well, Mr. Lincoln, if anybody had told me that in a great crisis like this, the people were going out to a little one-horse town and pick out a one-horse lawyer for President, I would not have believed it."

Mr. Lincoln was in the hands of the barber at the time. He whirled about in his chair, sweeping the man out of the way with his long arm. General Palmer suddenly realized the enormity of his blunder. But the President was not angry. Placing his hand on the general's knee he answered very earnestly, " Neither would I."

There is an illuminating entry in John Hay's diary. " B—— and the President continue to be on very good terms in spite of the publication of B.'s letter. . . . B. came to explain it to the President, but he told him he was too busy to quarrel with him. If he (B.) did n't show him the letter he probably would never see it."

Although he would not go half way toward a quarrel he would take a deal of

pains to correct a misunderstanding. He
relied much on a full and frank interchange
of ideas. He once wrote to Thurlow
Weed:

MY DEAR SIR: I have been brought to fear
recently that somehow by commission or
omission, I have caused you some degree of
pain. I have never entertained an unkind
feeling or a disparaging thought toward you,
and if I have said or done anything which
has been construed into such unkindness or
disparagement, it has been misconstrued. I
am sure if we could meet we would not part
with any unpleasant impression on either
side.

Carl Schurz sent him a letter of criticism
which he felt to be unjust, and to which he
sent a long and, for him, unusually caustic
reply. Mr. Schurz in his " Autobiography " tells the sequel:

Two or three days after Mr. Lincoln's
letter had reached me a special messenger

from him brought me another communication from him, a short note in his own hand, asking me to come to see him as soon as my duties would permit. He wished me, if possible, to call early in the morning before the usual crowd of visitors arrived. . . . The next morning at seven I reported myself at the White House. I was promptly shown into the little room upstairs which was at that time used for cabinet meetings — the room with the Jackson portrait above the mantelpiece — and found Mr. Lincoln seated in an arm-chair before the open grate fire, his feet in gigantic morocco slippers. He greeted me cordially as of old, and bade me pull up a chair and sit down by his side. Then he brought his large hand, with a slap, down on my knee, and said with a smile: " Now tell me, young man, whether you really think that I am as poor a fellow as you have made me out in your letter? "

I must confess this reception disconcerted me. I looked into his face and felt something like a big lump in my throat. After a while I gathered up my wits, and after a word of sorrow if I had written anything that could have pained him, I explained to him my impressions of the situation and my reasons for writing him as I had done. He listened with silent attention, and when I stopped said very seriously, "Well, I know that you are a warm antislavery man, and a good friend to me. Now let me tell you all about it." Then he unfolded in his peculiar way his views of the then existing state of affairs, his hopes and apprehensions, his troubles and his embarrassments, making many quaint remarks about men and things. I regret I cannot remember all. Then he described how the criticisms coming down upon all sides chafed him, and how my letter, although containing some points that were well founded and useful, had touched him as a terse summing-up of all the principal criticisms, and offered him a good chance at me for a reply. Then, slapping my knee again, he broke out in a loud laugh and exclaimed —

"Did n't I give it to you hard in my letter? Did n't I? But it did n't hurt, did it? I did not mean to, and therefore I wanted you to come so quickly."

He laughed again and seemed to enjoy the matter heartily. " Well," he added, " I guess we understand one another now, and it 's all right."

When after a conversation of more than an hour, I left him, I asked whether he still wished that I should write to him.

" Why certainly," he answered. " Write to me whenever the spirit moves you."

We parted better friends than ever.

More than once he wrote such letters, and then refrained from sending them. One of these was to General Meade after Lee's escape from Pennsylvania. Another, which was sent, bears an endorsement in his own hand.

" Withdrawn because considered harsh by General Halleck."

Still another, which came to light many years after the war, bore on its envelope in the handwriting of General Hunter, " The

President's reply to my 'ugly letter.'
This lay on his table a month after it was
written, and when finally sent was by a
special conveyance, with the direction that
it was only to be given me when I was in
a good humor."

While not insensible to personal criticism, he was far too even-tempered to be
unduly influenced by it. He knew that
much of it was like the Irishman's description of a tree-toad in one of his stories,
"Nothin' afther all but a blame noise!"
while some of the rest could be excused for
the reason given in another of his stories
by the henpecked man for standing his
wife's abuse, "It does n't hurt me any, and
you 've no idea what a power of good it
does to Sarah Ann."

He was broad-minded enough to remember that a man's opinion of him, or of his
administration, might not impair his usefulness as a public servant. It seemed a

poor rule that would not work both ways. He knew he would be censured, and rightly, for appointing a man to office simply because he praised him. It seemed equally illogical to refuse to appoint men simply because they blamed him. When he was remonstrated with for giving an office to one who had zealously opposed his reëlection, he is reported to have said, " That would not make him less fit for the place. And I think I have Scriptural authority for appointing him. You remember, when the Lord was on Mt. Sinai getting out a commission for Aaron, that same Aaron was at the foot of the mountain, making a false god for the people to worship. Yet Aaron got his commission."

His sense of fairness, and absolute freedom from personal resentment were nowhere more forcibly exhibited than in his relations with his generals. But clear reading of character went hand in hand with forbearance. His letter to General Joseph Hooker on placing him in command shows how completely this was so.

I have placed you at the head of the Army of the Potomac. Of course I have done this upon what appear to me to be sufficient reasons, and yet I think it best for you to know that there are some things in regard to which I am not quite satisfied with you. I believe you to be a brave and skilful soldier, which, of course, I like. I also believe you do not mix politics with your profession, in which you are right. You have confidence in yourself, which is a valuable, if not an indispensable quality. You are ambitious, which, within reasonable bounds, does good rather than harm; but I think that during General Burnside's command of the army you have taken counsel of your ambition and thwarted him as much as you could, in which you did a great wrong to the country, and to a most meritorious and honorable brother officer. I have heard, in such a way as to believe it, of your recently saying that both the army and the Government needed a dictator. Of course it was not for this, but in spite of it, that I have given you the command. Only those generals who gain successes can set up dictators. What I now ask of you is military success, and I will risk the dictatorship. The Government will support you to the utmost of its ability, which is neither more nor less than it has done and will do for all commanders. I much fear that the spirit which you have aided to infuse into the army, of criticizing their commander and withholding confidence from him, will now turn upon you. I shall assist you as far as I can to put it down. Neither you nor Napoleon, if he were alive again, could get any good out of an army while such a spirit prevails in it; and now, beware of rashness. Beware of rashness, but with energy and sleepless vigilance go forward and give us victories.

When Grant's critics brought up old gossip of his drunkenness, he answered with the jest which has been quoted as proof of his abandoned character, that he would be glad to know the brand of whisky he used; or with another variant of this same idea, quoted in Admiral Dahlgren's diary — the reply of George III to the charge that one of his generals was quite mad. " If that were true, he wished he would bite all his other generals."

One of Lincoln's secretaries, discussing the various generals, remarked that there was only one to whom power would be really dangerous. McClellan was too timid, Grant too sound and cool-headed to usurp authority, and so on. " Yes," said the President, referring to still another who had been mentioned. " He is like Jim Jett's brother. Jim used to say that his brother was the d—dst scoundrel that ever lived; but that in the infinite mercy of Providence, he was also the d—dst fool."

With McClellan the President's personal relations were typical. At first the general had been overwhelmed by his new and strange position, " President, General Scott and all deferring to me," but in contemplating his own great responsibility he quickly forgot this, and even the rights and courtesies due to others. The President, as was his custom, went freely to his house, by day or night. One evening a long and awkward youth, introduced as " Captain Orleans," just come to serve on McClellan's staff, went to announce his arrival. " One does n't like to make a messenger of the king of France, as that youth, the Count of Paris, would be, if his family had kept the throne," Lincoln said quietly, as he watched him mount the stairs.

But to McClellan the President's simplicity of manner seemed to indicate incompetence. Contemptuous mention of him and his cabinet in private letters passed to marks of open disrespect, which reached their climax one night when Mr. Lincoln, accompanied by Mr. Seward and a secretary, went to the general's house. Being told that he was at a wedding, they waited an hour for his return. They heard the servant at the door tell him that they were there, but the General paid scant heed, and passing the door of the room in which they sat, went on upstairs. After another half hour they sent to remind him that they were still waiting. Word came back that he had gone to bed.

No comment was made as the three walked away, but after Secretary Seward had been left at his own door the anger of the younger man blazed forth at this "unparalleled insolence of epaulettes." The President " seemed not to have noticed it specially, saying it was better at this time not to be making points of etiquette and personal dignity." But we are told that he stopped going to McClellan's house, sending for the General to come to him when he desired to see him.

It was harder for a man of Lincoln's temperament to forgive a wrong to his country than to himself; yet after McClel-

HIS FORGIVING SPIRIT

lan's dismal failure, after his wildly insubordinate letter charging the President and
the administration with doing their utmost
to sacrifice his army; and after his direct
suggestion that General Pope, who was in
peril through McClellan's own fault, be left
to " get out of his scrape as best he might,"
Lincoln crowded back all resentment public
and private, and over the protest of his
cabinet, placed him in command of the de-
fenses of Washington, because he was convinced that " if he cannot fight himself he
excels in making others ready to fight."

" We must use the tools we have," he
used to say. And his whole attitude was
summed up in his announcement, " I shall
do nothing in malice. What I deal with is
too vast for malicious dealing."

He understood McClellan, both his good
qualities and his defects. When he gave
Grant his commission as Lieutenant-Gen-
eral, the two had a little talk, and he spoke
a parable, telling of a war among the ani-

333

mals, when Jocco, the monkey, was sure he could command the army if only his tail were a little longer. So they spliced a piece on, and Jocco looked at it admiringly, and said he thought he would like a little more. And they gave it, and he called for more, until the room was full of tail. Then, there being no place elsewhere, they began coiling it about his shoulders, until the sheer weight of it broke him down.

Even when his sorrow and resentment were keenest he did not fail to give credit for the good which had been done. Lee's escape after Gettysburg grieved him sorely. He said to his son, " If I had gone up there I could have whipped them myself." He felt that at that moment the Union army held the war in the hollow of its hand — and would not close it. " Still," he added generously, " I am very, very grateful to Meade for the great service he did at Gettysburg."

When the Chief Justiceship, the highest

office in a President's gift, fell vacant, he gave it to Chase, though no one had worked harder to supplant Lincoln in the Presidency. The wonder and splendor of the act fairly dazzled the secretary who carried the nomination to the Senate.

"Congress met Monday," he wrote, "but the President did not get the message ready until Tuesday when it was sent in. At the same time he sent in the nomination of Chase for Chief Justice of the Supreme Court. Probably no other man than Lincoln would have had, in this age of the world, the degree of magnanimity to thus forgive and exalt a rival who had so deeply and unjustifiably intrigued against him. It is, however, only another marked illustration of the greatness of the President in this age of little men."

But his quiet appreciation of Chase's position had been very keen. During the interval between his resignation from the cabinet, and his appointment as Chief Justice,

335

ABRAHAM LINCOLN

Mr. Lincoln's secretary one day brought his chief a letter from Mr. Chase who was in Ohio.

"What is it about?" the President asked.

"Simply a kind and friendly letter."

Without reading it, Mr. Lincoln said, "File it with his other recommendations."

XVI

HIS REASON AND HIS HEART

THOUGH Lincoln's place in history rests on the fact that he freed the slaves, his place in the hearts of men rests on something entirely different — the way in which he did it. A fanatic, or a tyrant might have signed a proclamation of emancipation; but only a man of clear vision and surpassing goodness could have moved through years of bloodshed to a culminating act which destroyed millions of his countrymen's property at a stroke of the pen, and yet kept an ever warmer place in their affections.

His two qualities of head and heart acted like counterweights. His logic, though

unsparing, was never hopeless, being
warmed by the goodness of his heart. He
believed that right would ultimately triumph, and this gave him patience to move
slowly, to bear apparent defeat, and to
wait the appointed time of the Lord. His
faith in a mysterious overruling Providence was too sincere and too humble to
permit his attempting to force either righteousness or justice on an unready world.

Personal observation and experience had
very little to do in forming his convictions
on slavery. Though born in a slave State
he left it when a mere child, and he had
only passing glimpses of slavery's lights
and shadows during his two flatboat voy-
ages to New Orleans. It was his inborn
sense of natural justice which revolted
against the barbarous selfishness of the
system.

"If slavery is not wrong, nothing is
wrong," he said. To the argument that
it was a necessity forced upon the white

man, he replied, " that going many thousand miles, seizing a set of savages, bringing them here and making slaves of them,
is a necessity imposed on us by them, involves a species of logic to which my mind
will scarcely assent."

But he recognized that the problem had
long since passed that stage. In his
Peoria speech, when he stepped forth as
the champion of freedom, he frankly admitted that, " If all earthly power were
given me I should not know what to do as
to the existing institution. My first impulse would be to free all the slaves and
send them to Liberia, to their own native
land. But a moment's reflection would
convince me that whatever of high hope (as
I think there is) there may be in this in the
long run, its sudden execution is impossible.
If they were all landed there in a day they
would all perish in the next ten days."

Every actual observation deepened his
natural convictions. Yet he did not allow

his feelings to carry away his reason. He remembered that the practice was rooted in custom, and entrenched in constitution and law. To cut it out would be to endanger the national life. Also, while his heartfelt compassion went out to the slave, he had broad charity for the slave-holder, dominated by education, local prejudice and property interests.

This enabled him at the very beginning of his career to strike that key-note in statesmanship through which he wrought one of the world's great political reforms. He had been but two years in the legislature of Illinois when that body passed resolutions " highly disapproving abolition societies," and declaring that " the right of property in slaves is secured to the slaveholding States by the Federal Constitution," the identical proposition in support of which the South began civil war. Lincoln and five others voted against it. In addition, in order not to leave their sentiments in doubt, he and one other member signed a written protest and entered it on the journal, reciting their belief that the institution of slavery was founded on both injustice and bad policy, but that Congress had no power to interfere with it in the States, and that while it had power to abolish it in the District of Columbia, it ought only to exercise that power at the request of the people of the District.

Conservative as this seems, it required at that day a sturdy political courage to sign such a document, in face of the violent prejudice against everything savoring of " abolitionism." It was in that same year that a mob at Alton, Illinois, shot to death Elijah P. Lovejoy for persisting in his right to print an anti-slavery newspaper.

Twelve years afterward, during his term in Congress, Lincoln presented a bill for compensated emancipation — his plan for making the path of righteousness easier to the slave-owner, and the path toward liberty less dangerous for the slave. By its provisions masters were to receive money value for their property, and the slaves adequate guardianship and training for their new life. It could be accomplished only with the full consent of the owners, and he proposed to try it experimentally in the District of Columbia, a territory so small that its workings could be easily watched and any dangerous tendencies noted. The measure had the approval both of the conservative citizens of Washington, and of the anti-slavery leaders in Congress; but it failed to become a law, party heat being already too great to admit of moderate legislation. He could save neither sinned against nor sinners. In the poetic imagery of the Second Inaugural, it was decreed that the blood drawn by the lash must be paid for in blood drawn by the sword.

All Lincoln's study of the question during the years that separated his Peoria speech from his taking the oath of office as

President confirmed him in his early belief
that slavery was lawful in the Southern
States, and that where this was the case the
only remedy lay with the people living in
those States. All his effort was directed
toward preventing its spread into Federal
territory, where, he held, the Government
had a right to interfere. When he took
the oath as President he assumed the official responsibility of the judge, who cannot allow his individual feelings to supplant
the mandates of the law.

Then came the Civil War. If Lincoln
had been only a political theorist, he would
have taken this opportunity to declare that
by appealing to arms slavery had subjected
itself to the risks of war, and would have
at once launched against it his subsequent
decree of military emancipation. But his
education had made him first of all a practical statesman, and practical statesmanship demanded the maintenance of the integrity and power of the Union first of all.

Rash reforms like that proposed by Fremont and antislavery radicals would imperil the Union, and to permit the Union to die was to permit slavery to live. So, champion of freedom though he was, he annulled Fremont's proclamation.

His paramount duty he emphasized in his letter answering the criticisms of Horace Greeley.

As to the policy I " seem to be pursuing," as you say, I have not meant to leave any one in doubt. I would save the Union. I would save it the shortest way under the Constitution. . . . If there be those who would not save the Union unless they could at the same time destroy slavery, I do not agree with them. My paramount object in this struggle is to save the Union, and not either to save or to destroy slavery. . . . What I do about slavery and the colored race I do because I believe it helps to save the Union, and what I forbear I forbear because I do not believe it would help to save the Union.

HIS REASON AND HEART

I shall do less whenever I shall believe what I am doing hurts the cause, and I shall do more whenever I shall believe doing more will help the cause. . . . I have here stated my purpose according to my view of official duty; and I intend no modification of my oft-expressed personal wish that all men everywhere could be free.

He had a broader aim than mere conquest of the South. A true restoration of the Union must include a renewal of fraternal sympathy between the sections. In this spirit he recommended and Congress adopted his old policy of compensated abolishment — the offer of a money equivalent to States that would voluntarily relinquish slavery, holding it to be a remedy at once more effectual, more humane, and far less costly than war. The offer was refused, yet its spirit secured the adhesion of the border States to the Union, pushing the military frontier down from the Ohio River to the Tennessee line, and adding during the war more than 225,000 volunteers to the Union armies.

The rejection of this generous offer, and simultaneous reverses to McClellan's army before Richmond brought about the military necessity which justified Lincoln in using his authority as Commander-in-Chief of the army to issue his proclamation of military emancipation. Important as was this act, the signing of the decree was only an incident in the battle he was commissioned to wage, and about which he had recorded his well-considered resolve, " I expect to maintain this contest until successful, or till I die, or am conquered, or my term expires, or Congress or the country forsake me." The great issue was not the bondage of a race, but the life of a nation, a principle of government, a question of primary human right.

The country accepted the edict of emancipation as wise and necessary, but whether it would be held valid in law, Lincoln

frankly said he did not know. If the rebellion should triumph, manifestly the
proclamation would be so much waste paper. If the Union were victorious, every
step of that victory would be clothed with
the mantle of law. That was the lesson
of all history; the philosophy of government.

Of one thing he was sure. Having issued his proclamation he would never re-
tract or modify it. The freed slaves had
done their part. They had been armed
and had fought shoulder to shoulder with
the whites, bravely and well. To restore
the Union with their help, under a pledge
of liberty, and then, under whatever legal
construction, to attempt to reënslave them,
would be a moral monstrosity — would be,
in the language of one of his early
speeches, " to repeal human nature."
" There have been men base enough to propose to me to return to slavery our black
warriors of Port Hudson and Olustee," he

said. " Should I do so, I should deserve to be damned in time and eternity."

He wished the voluntary consent of the States to his act, and therefore set in motion the machinery of a constitutional amendment. Lincoln did not live to see it a part of the Constitution, but it became so less than a year after his death.

These measures, taken in orderly sequence, in strict pursuance of duty, had brought about through his agency the end he desired and thought so very far away. His reason might well have been satisfied. But his heart was not yet content. As the war drew to its close his kindness went out more and more to these enemies who were yet brothers. When he met the Confederate commissioners at Hampton Roads, and through his sympathy and intuition divined their undercurrent of hopelessness, he told them that he personally would favor payment by the Federal Government of a liberal indemnity for the loss of slave property, on absolute cessation of the war, and voluntary abolition of slavery in the Southern States.

He spent the day after his return from this meeting in perfecting a new proposal designed as a peace offering to the South, and that evening called his cabinet together and read them the draft of a joint resolution and a proclamation offering the Southern States $400,000,000 on condition that the Thirteenth Amendment be ratified by the requisite number of States before July first, 1865. But this was a height of altruism to which his constitutional advisers could not follow him. " You are all opposed to me," he said sadly, as he folded the paper and ended the discussion. But he still continued to ponder offers of friendship. In the last public speech he made, to a crowd of people gathered in front of the Executive Mansion to celebrate Grant's victory, he hinted at some new announcement he was considering and would soon make to the South. Can it be doubted it was as generous as this one?

Such, in a broad way, were Lincoln's achievements and action on slavery. He wrought in the great field of original statesmanship, and the Archimedean lever whereby he moved the world was public opinion. Under his guidance, in the swift rush of events, results came to pass in a decade that had seemed like hopes a hundred years removed. For this he took to himself no credit. " I claim not to have controlled events," he said, " but frankly admit that events have controlled me." And again, " My policy is to have no policy." Keeping in view his large ideal and ultimate aim, he disposed of each individual problem as it came up, though this led him into the apparent inconsistency of refusing to arm negro soldiers, then of arming them, of revoking military proclamations of emancipation, then of issuing a great and sweeping edict of freedom —

once it led him into actually offering to buy a slave for $500.

Lincoln's reply to the minister who anxiously " hoped the Lord was on his side," summed up his creed and his practice. He said that did not trouble him in the least. His great concern was that he and the country should be on the side of the Lord.

Mention has been made of Lincoln's extreme reluctance to approve the death penalty. This was not the outcome of sentimental regard for soldiers. In 1862 a very serious Indian uprising with atrocious massacres took place in Minnesota. After it was quelled a court-martial tried the prisoners, and under the impulse of popular indignation sentenced about three hundred to be hanged. Learning of this the President ordered the execution stayed, and the testimony forwarded to him. Letters and telegrams poured in upon him, begging him to allow the sentences to stand; but determined to have no hasty sac-

rifice, he patiently investigated each case
for himself, finally confirming the sentences
of less than forty out of the three hundred,
these being cases where reliable witnesses
testified to seeing the men actually engaged in acts of atrocity. In forward-
ing the testimony to the Senate he stated
his anxiety " to not act with so much clemency as to encourage another outbreak on
the one hand, nor with so much severity as
to be real cruelty on the other."

For red and white alike he stood firm in
his determination to execute only the de-
crees of justice.

" In considering the policy to be
adopted for suppressing the insurrection
I have been anxious and careful that the
inevitable conflict for this purpose shall
not degenerate into a violent and remorse-
less revolutionary struggle," he told Congress in his first annual message. Both his
reason and his heart forbade him to sanction measures of retaliation urged for the

massacre of negro soldiers at Fort Pillow. Frederick Douglas, the colored man, with whom he talked on this subject, said, " I shall never forget the benignant expression of his face, the tearful look of his eye, and the quiver of his voice." He could not take men out and kill them in cold blood for what was done by others. " Once begun," he said, " I do not know where such a measure would stop."

The same question came up in regard to the treatment of prisoners, and received the same answer. It was argued that if men were starved at Libby Prison and Andersonville, the same treatment should be meted out to Confederates. " Whatever others may say or do I never can, and I never will, be accessory to such treatment of human beings," he said.

The question of prisoners lay heavy on his heart. General Butler told of a day when the President was visiting his command. They had gone through the hospitals, and the wards of wounded Confederate prisoners, and he had brought light and cheer by his presence. Afterward as they sat at dinner he was weary and depressed. The General was pained to see that his guest did not eat, and asked if he were ill. "I am well enough," he replied, pushing away his plate, "but would to God this dinner or provisions like it were with our poor prisoners in Andersonville."

As the war drew to its close the questions of exchanging prisoners, and of the treatment of Southern leaders, assumed larger proportions. Secretary Welles, who found time to write many things in his "deadly diary," moralized thus:

This war is extraordinary in all its aspects and phases, and no man is prepared to meet them. . . . I have often thought that greater severity might well be exercised, and yet it would tend to barbarism. No traitor has been hung. I doubt if there will be; but an

example should be made of some of the leaders, for present and for future good. They
may, if taken, be imprisoned, or driven into
exile, but neither would be lasting. Parties
would form for their relief, and ultimately
succeed in restoring the worst of them to
their homes and the privileges they originally
enjoyed. Death is the proper penalty and
atonement. . . . But I apprehend there will
be very gentle measures in closing up the
rebellion.

He knew his chief. The full difference
in their mental make-up is shown in an entry in this same diary four months later.
" Oct. 5, 1864. The President came to see
me pretty early this morning in relation
to the exchange of prisoners. It had
troubled him during the night."

Lincoln's care was not how to make the
punishment lasting, but how best to heal
the scars of war. An endorsement on a
paper that passed between him and the
War Department shows his whole attitude.

"On principle I dislike an oath which requires a man to swear he has not done wrong. It rejects the Christian principle of forgiveness on terms of repentance. I think it is enough if the man does no wrong hereafter."

He frankly admitted that he hoped the leaders of the rebellion would escape. "If you have an elephant on your hands, and he wants to run away — better let him run!" he said. And with similar intent he told the story of a boy who, with much expenditure of time and energy had acquired a coon, only to find him a great nuisance. He could not, however, bring himself to admit this to his family. One day, leading it along the road, he had more than he could do to manage the little vixen. At length, with clothes torn, and muscles weary, he sank to the ground, tired out. A gentleman passing, asked what was the matter.

"Oh, this coon is such a trouble to me."

"Why don't you get rid of him, then?"

"Hush," said the boy. "Don't you see, he is gnawing his rope off? That is just what I want. I'm going to let him do it, and then I can go home and tell the folks he got away from me."

On April 11 Lincoln spoke from a window of the White House to a large and joyful crowd, gathered in honor of Lee's surrender. The President's speech was full of conciliation. Senator Harlan followed, and in the course of his remarks, touched on the thought uppermost in everybody's mind. "What shall we do with the rebels?" he asked. A voice answered from the crowd, "Hang them!"

Lincoln's small son was in the room, playing with the pens on the table. Looking up he caught his father's pained expression.

"No, no, Papa," he cried in his childish voice. "Not hang them. Hang on to them!"

ABRAHAM LINCOLN

"That is it! Tad has got it. We must hang on to them!" the President exclaimed in triumph.

Lincoln's final official act was writing, "Let it be done," on the petition of a Confederate prisoner who desired to take the oath of allegiance. "I think this will take precedence of Stanton," he is reported to have said, for Stanton wished to hedge rehabilitation about with more safeguards.

In the cabinet meeting on that last morning of his life he talked in a strain of the utmost friendliness toward the South. No one need expect him to take any part in hanging these men, even the worst of them. Enough lives had been sacrificed. Anger must be put aside.

With words like these on his lips, and a gladness in his heart which found expression in a physical embrace of his rough and prickly friend Stanton, he closed their last cabinet session.

358

XVII

L INCOLN knew no foreign tongue, yet he spoke two languages — the vernacular, and a strong, majestic prose, akin to poetry. He used one and then the other, as best suited his audience or the nature of his subject; but whatever the language, it expressed high aims, for he had only one moral code.

Growing up among very simple people, he acquired a plainness of manner, both in thought and speech, which differentiated him, all his days, from the statesmen nurtured in ease and plenty. The Boston *Transcript*, commenting on his first inaugural, called it " the plain homespun language of a man of the people, who was accustomed to talk with ' the folks,' "—" the language of a man of vital common sense, whose words exactly fitted his facts and thoughts."

This simplicity shocked not a few. It was not living up to the popular conception of a statesman. The echoes wakened by our great orators were still rolling over the land, and every budding politician was expected to rival them. A soaring peroration was deemed as essential to a speech as the " Fellow citizens " with which it opened. Lincoln, with his straightforward sentences made up of short forceful words, was not playing the game according to accepted rules. Ex-president Tyler complained that he did not even play it according to rules of grammar.

In his later years Lincoln used to repeat with glee the picturesque description of a Southwestern orator who " mounted the rostrum, threw back his head, shined his

eyes, opened his mouth, and left the consequences to God." This was an exercise of
faith in which he never indulged, though he
passed through a period of using the
rather florid eloquence of the stump speech
with great effect. Studies in the law encourage neither flights of fancy nor misuse
of words. His scrupulous regard for
truth, and his own good sense, speedily
corrected any leaning toward extravagant
metaphor.

In one of Lincoln's early speeches in
New England he expressed a " feeling of
real modesty " in addressing an audience
" this side the mountains," where everybody was supposed to be instructed and
wise. He had the unschooled man's wist-
ful admiration and longing for educational
advantages which had been denied him;
and until convinced by contact and much
experience with men trained in the best
routine machines of learning, actually expected to suffer by comparison. It is quite

possible that up to the very last he was astonished, and a bit disappointed to find that he held his own so well beside them.

He had, too, the genuine admiration for the arts and for science common to many Westerners whose taste and appreciation have outrun their opportunities, and he enjoyed talking with men of these pursuits — looking, as it were, through their eyes into a world so different from his own. Professor Joseph Henry was one of the rare men in Washington in those days. The two were mutually attracted, though too busy to see much of each other. The scientist was astonished at the President's intelligent grasp of subjects about which he professed entire ignorance. " He is producing a powerful impression upon me," he confessed, " more powerful than any one I can now recall. It increases with every interview. I think it my duty to take philosophic views of men and things, but the President upsets me. If I did not resist the inclination, I might even fall in love with him." Lincoln on his side admitted that until meeting Professor Henry he supposed the Smithsonian to be a rather useless institution. "But," he said, " it must be a grand school if it produces such thinkers as he."

The President was fond of music, in a frank untutored way, though he had not an excruciatingly sensitive ear. The clash of regimental bands playing against each other, which drove Colonel Baker to distraction at a certain review, did not disturb him in the least. Perhaps it is better to say that he liked the idea of music — the sound and swing of martial tunes, and the pathos of a simple ballad. He must have been unconsciously sensitive to rhythm, for he read poetry uncommonly well, and his own prose at its best has a movement as inevitable as that of a marching column.

There is a popular saying that only

ABRAHAM LINCOLN

three books are needed to complete a library — the Bible, Blackstone and Shakspere. He had delved deep in all three.
His lawyer's training is visible in everything he wrote, down to the smallest scrap,
in a clearness of expression which leaves
no chance for misunderstanding either the
fact stated or his own motive. But it has,
too, that indefinable literary elegance
called style. In the sentence quoted in the
last chapter, for instance, " I expect to
maintain this contest until successful, or
till I die, or am conquered, or my term expires, or Congress or the country forsake
me," no possible lawyer-loophole is left unguarded, yet because of its diction it is
neither redundant nor ungraceful.

His familiarity with and use of Biblical
phraseology was remarkable even in a time
when such use was more common than now.
We are told that he read Shakspere more
than all other writers put together. When
only two or three were present he was fond

of reading aloud from the tragedies or the historical plays. John Hay tells us that " he passed many of the summer evenings in this way when occupying his cottage at the Soldiers' Home. . . . the plays he most affected were ' Hamlet,' ' Macbeth,' and the series of histories. Among these he never tired of ' Richard II.' The terrible outburst of grief and despair into which Richard falls in the third act had a peculiar fascination for him." Mr. Hay heard him read it at Springfield, at the White House, and at the Soldiers' Home.

For God's sake, let us sit upon the ground
And tell sad stories of the death of kings: —
How some have been deposed; some slain in
    war;
Some haunted by the ghosts they have de-
    posed;
Some poison'd by their wives, some sleeping
    kill'd;
All murdered: for within the hollow crown
That rounds the mortal temples of a king

Keeps Death his court; and there the antic
    sits,
Scoffing his state, and grinning at his pomp,
Allowing him a breath, a little scene,
To monarchize, be fear'd, and kill with
    looks,
Infusing him with self and vain conceit,
As if this flesh, which walls about our life,
Were brass impregnable, and humor'd thus
Comes at the last and with a little pin
Bores through the castle walls, and — fare-
    well, king!

He liked to see these same plays acted.
Apparently he cared more for the acting
of men than of women — more for Hackett, for instance, than for Charlotte Cush-
man. He was so delighted with Hackett's
Falstaff that he wrote the veteran actor a
letter, which through an indiscretion on
the latter's part, was printed in the New
York *Herald* with accompanying abuse.
Hackett, greatly mortified, made profound
apologies, to which the President replied

in the kindest manner, that though he had
not expected to see his note in print, it had
not distressed him. " These comments
constitute a fair specimen of what has occurred to me through life. I have endured
a great deal of ridicule without much malice and have received a great deal of kindness not quite free from ridicule. I am
used to it."

He told a friend that he had never read
a whole novel in his life, though he once
began " Ivanhoe." Occasionally he read a
scientific work with deep interest, but his
busy life left him little time for such indul-
gence. During his Presidency the little
leisure that he had for reading was devoted, almost of necessity, to works on
military science.

" The music of Lincoln's thought was
always in a minor key," my father wrote.
Of modern poems the sad or reminiscent
appealed to him — like Holmes's " Last
Leaf," Hood's " Haunted House," and

ABRAHAM LINCOLN

"Oh, why should the spirit of mortal be proud?"

Among his own writings are found a few bits of verse. On the Day of Judgment few indeed will be the public men who will not have to face a similar charge. Lincoln's verses were inspired by revisiting his old home, "within itself as unpoetical as any spot on the earth," he admitted, but which "aroused feelings in me which were certainly poetry, though whether my expression of these feelings is poetry, is quite another question."

Certain other fragments — one on Niagara Falls, notes for a law lecture, and a more extended paper, the skeleton, partly clothed, of a lecture on "Discoveries, Inventions and Improvements," which he delivered a few times in Springfield and neighboring towns in 1859 and 1860, are all that we have of his efforts at self expression on subjects other than his controlling inspiration.

LINCOLN THE WRITER

One who heard the lecture described it as longer and containing several fine passages not in the printed copy. It is easy to see that even as it stands, Lincoln's smile and manner would have made another thing of it. Even in print there are a few bits wittily his own, like the characterization of Young America — " He owns a large part of the world by right of possessing it, and all the rest by right of wanting it and intending to have it."

The probability is that all these were composed within that period of comparative leisure between the end of his term in Congress and the day when the repeal of the Missouri Compromise unchained the new political controversy. He attached no undue importance to them. Refusing an invitation to lecture in the spring of 1859, he wrote: " I cannot do so now. I must stick to the courts awhile. I read a sort of lecture to three different audiences during the last month and this, but I did

so under circumstances which made it a
waste of no time whatever."

At what time Lincoln began the compo-
sition of his first inaugural was unknown,
even to his secretary. My father's opinion was that while he did not set himself
seriously to this task until the result of the
election had been ascertained beyond
doubt, it is quite possible that it had been
considered with great deliberation during
the summer, and that sentences and perhaps paragraphs of it had been put in
writing. Mr. Lincoln often resorted to
the process of cumulative thought, and his
constant tendency to and great success in
axiomatic definition resulted in a large
measure from a habit he had of reducing
a forcible idea to writing, and keeping it
till further reasoning enabled him to elaborate or conclude his point or argument.
There were many of these scraps among
his papers — seldom in the shape of mere

rough notes; almost always as a finished proposition or statement.

It was about one of his political letters, the Conkling letter of August 26, 1863, that John Hay wrote to my father with irrepressible youthful enthusiasm:

" His last letter is a great thing. Some hideously bad rhetoric . . . yet the whole letter takes its solid place in history as the great utterance of a great man. The whole cabinet could not have tinkered up a letter which could have compared with it. He can snake a sophism out of its hole better than all the trained logicians of all schools. I do not know whether the nation is worthy of him. . . ."

This Conkling letter has been called " his last stump speech." It has in it all the qualities which made him the leader of his party in Illinois for a generation — the close reasoning, the innate perception of political conduct, wit, sarcasm, and

that picturesque eloquence which abounded
in his earlier and more careless oratory.
But all are strengthened and intensified
by a sense of his great responsibility.
" The Father of Waters again goes un-
vexed to the sea," " All the watery mar-
gins " of our land, and " Man's vast future," with their poetic note, are balanced
by statements as irrefutable as that two
and two make four, and his axiom that
" there can be no appeal from the ballot
to the bullet "— Nowhere a syllable that
could be dispensed with, nowhere a word
lacking.

Modest as he was, Lincoln knew the
value of his work. When a friend asked
him if he meant to attend the mass meeting
in Springfield to which Mr. Conkling's letter was an invitation, he replied,

" No. I shall send them a letter instead, and it will be a rather good letter."

Although a ready impromptu speaker,
he made for himself a rule to which he ad-

hered during his Presidency. This was to say nothing in public that he had not first committed to writing. Reprimands to delinquent officials, the little speech on presenting Grant his commission as Lieutenant General, and the speeches of formal ceremony to diplomats, as well as the far more intimate lecture to his cabinet, were all carefully written beforehand.

When he delivered the Gettysburg Address he held the paper in his hand, but did not read from it. It was " in a firm free way, with more grace than is his wont " that he " said his half dozen lines of consecration." " And the music wailed, and we went home through crowded and cheering streets — and all the particulars are in the daily papers," John Hay wrote.

Next day Edward Everett sent the President a note of thanks for personal courtesies received, and of appreciation of the address. " I should be glad if I could flatter myself that I had come as near the central idea of the occasion in two hours as you did in two minutes."

Mr. Lincoln answered, " In our respective parts yesterday you could not have been excused to make a short address, nor I a long one. I am pleased to know that in your judgment, the little I did say was not entirely a failure. Of course I knew Mr. Everett would not fail."

Much has been written to prove that neither Lincoln nor the country was satisfied with the address, and that it was reserved for English critics to discover its wonderful beauty. The only direct evidence lies in this letter to Edward Everett, which may or may not conceal more meaning than a conventional answer to a merited compliment. The probability is that though he thought the address not nearly so bad as some would have us imagine, he did not dream that the world would acclaim it a masterpiece. He would doubtless have been astonished, and the first to protest, had he been told that he was a great writer. Yet the world so holds him; and surely in elevation of thought and nobility of expression it is hard to find his superior.

Sherman called his style " the unaffected and spontaneous eloquence of the heart." It was indeed an eloquence of the heart. His early striving after lucid brevity, and his dramatic sense, gave him the power of expressing ideas in short and forceful terms. His moral purpose made him a teacher whose voice carried far. To this he had attained before he became President. But it was the experience of the Presidency which brought to full flower another quality, a beauty of phrase and a benignity of expression only hinted at in his earlier writings.

" We shall nobly save or meanly lose, the last, best hope of earth." " It is rather for us to be here dedicated to the great task remaining before us — that from these honored dead we take increased devotion to that cause for which they gave the last full measure of devotion." "I have not willingly planted a thorn in any man's bosom." "We must not sully victory with harshness." "With malice toward none; with charity for all; with firmness in the right as God gives us to see the right, let us strive on to finish the work we are in, to bind up the nation's wounds; to care for him who shall have borne the battle, and for his widow, and his orphan — to do all which may achieve and cherish a just and lasting peace among ourselves, and with all nations."

Before his election he might have written, "Fellow citizens, we cannot escape history!" But he could not have spoken the "half dozen lines of consecration" at Gettysburg, or the marvelous words of the Second Inaugural.

It was his suffering — the thorny path he trod, carrying a nation's grief, which gave his words their final majesty.

XVIII

A FEW characters live in history un-circumscribed by time or place. They may have died ten centuries or ten days ago; we feel them to be as vital and as modern as ourselves.

It is hard to think of Lincoln in any environment except our own, yet the country he knew was vastly different. The Civil War bridged a gulf wider than we realize. Up to that time America had been the land of individual effort, where those who were dissatisfied could go on into the wilderness and work out their doom or their salvation unmolested. The very peopling of the continent had been a protest against

despotism — against doing things the way
some one else decreed. In our early attempts at concerted government concessions toward central power were given
grudgingly, and sometimes withdrawn
again, in spite of demonstrated success.
We accepted the motto, " In union is
strength," officially; in private we pinned
our faith to its opposite — " every man
for himself."

By its mere magnitude the Civil War
compelled a change. The struggle assumed such vast proportions that Americans were forced to think in a new way —
to do things together in large masses, to
contemplate immense quantities, to calcu-
late stupendous sums.

A volunteer army is in essence coöperation, and four years' training in the possibilities of voluntary coöperation taught
the nation the value of " team work." At
the end of the struggle over a million men,
trained in these new ways, carried their

knowledge back into civil life, and spread it through the business world. If the germ of secession lay hidden in the hold of the Dutch slaver that sailed up the James River in 1619, the inception of present industrial methods was breathed in by both Union and Confederate armies as they lay in the swamps of Virginia.

Just enough poison may be a tonic, though too much is a deadly drug. Individualism did its great work on this continent, but, pushed to its conclusion, would have brought ruin. This new force quickened the pulse of national life so that the waste of war was repaired with unheard-of speed; and now men wonder how much farther it is wise to pursue the same course.

Remembering the wisdom of Lincoln who presided over the other great change, people have sought to make him a prophet for this generation. Not finding what they wanted among his words, the unscrupulous have not hesitated to invent them. My father once made a list of a dozen or more spurious quotations and allegations concerning Lincoln; but the one he was most often called upon to deny, was this:

Yes, we can all congratulate ourselves that this cruel war is drawing to a close. It has cost a vast amount of treasure and blood. The best blood of the flower of American youth has been freely offered upon our country's altar that the nation might live. It has been a trying hour for the republic, but I see in the near future a crisis arising which unnerves me and causes me to tremble for the safety of my country. As a result of the war, corporations have been enthroned, and an era of corruption in high places will follow, and the money power of the country will endeavor to prolong its reign by working upon the prejudices of the people until all wealth is aggregated in a few hands and the republic is destroyed. I feel at this time more anxiety for the safety of my country than ever before, even in the midst of the war. God grant that my fears may prove groundless!

This alleged quotation seems to have made its first appearance in the Presidential campaign of 1888, and it has returned with planetary regularity ever since. Although convinced by internal evidence of its falsity, my father made every effort to trace it to its source, but could find no responsible or respectable clue. The truth is that Lincoln was no prophet of a distant day. His heart and mind were busy with the problems of his own time. The legacy he left his countrymen was not the warning of a seer, but an example and an obligation to face their own dark shadows with the sanity and courageous independence he showed in looking upon those that confronted him.

His early life was essentially of the old era. He made his own career by individual effort. His childhood, on the edge of civilization, had on the one side the freedom of the wilderness, and on the other the very few simple things which have been garnered as necessities from the world's useless belongings. His lawyer's earnings, at their highest, were only a pittance, by modern estimate; and a hundred details of his letters and daily life — like his invitation to an audience in the Lincoln-Douglas campaign, to meet him " at candle-light," which was not a figure of speech but an actual condition, showed how completely he was part of that vanished time.

Yet when the change came he led the country out of old ways into new. Rising above the hatred and bitterness of the struggle, he held attention to the great and enduring principles which made such a sacrifice of life not only tolerable, but holy. By force of his own personality he shamed men into contempt for vindictiveness and meanness; and doing so, robbed war of its bitterest sting.

His sudden elevation to the Presidency had no deteriorating effect upon his qualities of head or of heart. His mental equipoise remained undisturbed, his moral sensitiveness unblunted, his simplicity of manner unchanged, his strong individuality untouched. His responsibilities served only to clear his judgment, confirm his courage and broaden and deepen his humanity.

Dwellers on mountain tops are lonely. The very clearness of his mind, and the largeness of his view, conspired to rob him of companionship in the sense of intellectual equality. A vainer man might have felt this. Lincoln, entirely without egotism, grasped the greater fact of human brotherhood, and found interest and companionship in the fact of a common humanity.

He had no false pride about little

things; no false modesty about great ones. He knew that he had a great part to play, and played it simply, earnestly. He had no illusions but also, no bitterness. He did have strong affections, a very real craving for sympathy, a merry wit, and an infinite capacity for pain. He was a man of patience, of faith, of broad principles, of high aspirations; accepting without rude rebuff any good he could secure for the moment, yet all the while shaping and preparing in meditation and silent hope the path by which the nation might mount to higher levels.

This man of no illusions lived very close to mystery. From the day he stood beside his father in the unhealthful shade of Pigeon Cove, a little heart-sick boy, watching the whip-saw eat its way through the green wood that was to make coffins for his mother and the others who had died of the dreadful " milk sickness," to the night before he was murdered, when he dreamed again his recurrent dream of the strange ship hurrying toward a dark and unknown shore, he seemed always to feel the unseen very near.

Every act of his private life, and every public paper he sent forth, testified not only to his belief in, but to his reliance upon, a power higher and wiser than himself. " The purposes of the Almighty are perfect and must prevail," he wrote, " though we erring mortals may fail to accurately perceive them in advance. . . . We shall yet acknowledge His wisdom and our own error therein. Meanwhile we must work earnestly in the best lights He gives us, trusting that so working still conduces to the great end He ordains."

In its reverence for the words and acts of Christ the civilized world has set up its standard of moral philosophy. Judged by this standard Lincoln must be accorded preëminence among his contem-

25   385

ABRAHAM LINCOLN

poraries. A patriot in his complete
devotion to his Government and its Constitution, his greatness of soul rose above
patriotism and acknowledged the right of
every human being made in God's image
to his personal act of kindness and mercy
— not as an act of grace from a mighty
ruler, as he was; but as a service commanded alike by the laws of man and God.
In the practice of justice, of patriotism,
of mercy — in the utter oblivion of self,
" with malice toward none, with charity
for all," he followed in the footsteps of
the Galilean.

Fate placed him at the cross-roads of
national destiny. The muse of history
thrust before him a blank tablet and bade
him write upon it the life or death of the
New World republic. It is our privilege
to read from that tablet the record of a
Union preserved, and a new conception of
dominion, majesty and power, tempered
by the Golden Rule. But at that time no

386

HIS MORAL FIBER

mortal, not even he who was to write, could foretell the inscription. He himself did not pretend to pierce the veil of the future. He only knew the magnitude of his task, and that he was not dismayed.

THE END